BTEC
FIRST
AWARD

SPORT

ALWAYS LEARNING

PEARSON

Published by Pearson Education Limited, Edinburgh Gate, Harlow, Essex, CM20 2JE.

www.pearsonschoolsandfecolleges.co.uk

Text © Pearson Education Limited 2012
Typeset by Phoenix Photosetting, Chatham, Kent, UK
Original illustrations © Pearson Education Limited 2012
Illustrated by Vicky Woodgate, Phoenix Photosetting and Oxford Designers and Illustrators
Picture research by Harriet Merry and Caitlin Swain
Front cover photos: © Getty Images: OJO Images/Paul Bradbury
Indexing by Indexing Specialists (UK) Ltd.

The rights of Mark Adams, Adam Gledhill and Pam Phillippo to be identified as authors of this work
have been asserted by them in accordance with the Copyright, Designs and Patents Act 1988.

First published 2012.

16 15 14 13
10 9 8 7 6 5 4 3 2

British Library Cataloguing in Publication Data
A catalogue record for this book is available from the British Library

ISBN 978 1 446905 55 5

Printed in the UK at Ashford Colour Press, Gosport, Hants

Websites
There are links to relevant websites in this book. In order to ensure that the links are up to date,
that the links works, and that the sites aren't inadvertently links to sites that could be considered
offensive, we have made the links available on our website at www.pearsonhotlinks.co.uk. Search for
the title BTEC First Sport Award Student Book or ISBN 978 1 446905 55 5.

Copies of official specifications for all Pearson qualifications may be found on: www.edexcel.com

A note from the publisher
In order to ensure that this resource offers high quality support for the associated BTEC qualification,
it has been through a review process by the awarding organisation to confirm that it fully covers the
teaching and learning content of the specification or part of a specification at which it is aimed, and
demonstrates an appropriate balance between the development of subject skills, knowledge and
understanding, in addition to preparation for assessment.

While the publishers have made every attempt to ensure that advice on the qualification and its
assessment is accurate, the official specification and associated assessment guidance materials are
the only authoritative source of information and should always be referred to for definitive guidance.

No material from an endorsed book will be used verbatim in any assessment set by BTEC.

Endorsement of a book does not mean that the book is required to achieve this BTEC qualification,
nor does it mean that it is the only suitable material available to support the qualification, and
any resource lists produced by the awarding organisation shall include this and other appropriate
resources.

Acknowledgements

The publisher would like to thank the following for their kind permission to reproduce their photographs:

(Key: b-bottom; c-centre; l-left; r-right; t-top)

Alamy Images: Aflo Alto 75c, Allstar Picture Library 59c, Corbis Bridge 121tl, Jonathan Goldberg 149c, Science Photo Library 112c, STEVE LINDRIDGE 107c; **Corbis:** Steve Bardens 56cr, Philip Brown 4bl, Nick Dolding 146c, Elizabeth Kreutz 125tl, Erik Isakson / Blend Image 8bl, Image Source 10cl, Mika 22b, Tim Tadder 110br; **Getty Images:** AFP 65tr, Shaun Botterill 91tc, Comstock Images 11tr, David Rogers 100cr, Getty Images 6cr, Laurence Griffiths 156br, Bertrand Guay / AFP 89c, Isaac Koval 172br, Chris Jackson 84br, Glyn Kirk / AFP 153br, Bryn Lennon 78c, Michael Regan 156tl, Mike Hewitt 88bc, Hans Neleman 169tc, Mark Nolan 70cl, Richard Langdon 64bl, Robert Cianflone 21cr, Scott Barbour 131cl, Andrew Wong 92c; **Glow Images:** Image 100. Corbis 94br; **Hawk-Eye Innovations Limited:** 62cl; **Imagestate Media:** John Foxx Collection 165bc; **John Foxx Images:** Imagestate 38c; **London 2012:** 47; **Pearson Education Ltd:** 27c, 45br, 123tr; **Photolibrary. com:** BananaStock 161t, Les and Dave Jacobs 19cr, Somos 67tr; **Rex Features:** 137tl; **Science Photo Library Ltd:** Living Art Enterprises 115c; **Shutterstock.com:** Andresr 132bl, 165tl, Andrey Shadrin 76tl, Ariwasabi 113tr, Auremar 133tr, Avava 119cl, Diego Barbieri 103c, Blazej Lyjak 129b, 130t, 132t, 134t, 136t, 139tr, 141tr, 142t, 144t, 146t, Adam Borkowski 101tr, Kris Butler 17c, Herminia Lucia Lopes Serra de Casais 60cr, Catalin Petolea 104tl, corepics 77b, 78t, 80t, 82t, 84t, 86t, 89tr, 90t, 93t, 94t, 97tr, 98t, Istvan Csak 111b, Dmitry Berkut 5tl, Elena Elisseeva 46bl, EpicStockMedia 18bl, Foodpics 56bl, Fotokostic 151b, 152t, 155tr, 157tr, 160t, 163tr, 164t, 166t, 168t, 170t, 173tr, Galina Barskaya 131c, Gelpi 48tl, Herbert Kratky 131cr, Huntstock.com 148bl, hxdbzxy 93cr, IKO 126bl, Jason Stitt 63tr, Josh Brown 97c, katania82 158bl, Kzenon 4t, 6t, 9tr, 10t, 12t, 14t, 17t, 18t, 20t, 22t, 25tr, 26t, 29tr, 31tr, 33tr, 35tr, 37tr, 39tr, 41tr, 127c, 141cr, lenetstan 2bl, Lucky Business 142br, John Lumb 137br, Monkey Business Images 159tr, 163tl, muzsy 114cl, naluwan 102bl, Natursports 71bc, 158tl, Nicole Weiss 7cl, Olga Besna 52bl, Pavel Shchegolev 168cl, Raphael Daniaud 108cr, Rob Marmion 128tl, Galushko Sergey 60cl, Dmitriy Shironosov 16tl, .shock 44tr, 105b, 106t, 108t, 111tr, 114t, 117tr, 118t, 121tr, 122t, 125tr, .shock 44tr, 105b, 106t, 108t, 111tr, 114t, 117tr, 118t, 121tr, 122t, 125tr, Smith&Smith 166cl, sportgraphic 51cr, 80cl, 81b, 85tr, 116tl, Stefan Schurr 98cr, Stephen Mcsweeny 147tc, Supri Suharjoto 74bl, Konstantin Sutyagin 140c, Suzanne Tucker 150tl, thelefty 154bc, Tim Hester Photography 100cl, wavebreakmedia ltd 24tl, xc 49br, 50t, 52t, 55tr, 56t, 58t, 60t, 64t, 66t, 68t, 70t, 72t, Yeko Photo Studio 3c **Veer/Corbis:** lightpoet 12bl

Cover images: *Front:* **Getty Images:** OJO Images / Paul Bradbury

All other images © Pearson Education

Picture Research by: Harriet Merry, Caitlin Swain

Every effort has been made to trace the copyright holders and we apologise in advance for any unintentional omissions. We would be pleased to insert the appropriate acknowledgement in any subsequent edition of this publication.

The author and publisher would like to thank the following individuals and organisations for permission to reproduce their materials:

p. 28 Aerobic endurance results table. Adapted, with permission, from Luc A. Léger, 1982, 'A Maximal Multistage Fitness Test to Predict VO$_2$Max', European Journal of Applied Physiology and Occupational Physiology, 1-12

p. 31 Forestry non-adjusted aerobic fitness values for males table. Adapted, with permission, from B.J. Sharkey, 1984, Physiology of Fitness, 2nd ed. (Champaign, IL: Human Kinetics), 258

p. 32 Forestry non-adjusted aerobic fitness values for females table. Adapted, with permission, from B.J. Sharkey, 1984, Physiology of Fitness, 2nd ed. (Champaign, IL: Human Kinetics), 259

p. 32 Forestry age-adjusted aerobic fitness values table. Adapted, with permission, from B.J. Sharkey, 1984, Physiology of Fitness, 2nd ed. (Champaign, IL: Human Kinetics), 260-61

p. 33 Forestry aerobic fitness values table. Adapted, with permission, from B.J. Sharkey, 1984, Physiology of Fitness, 2nd ed. (Champaign, IL: Human Kinetics), 262

p. 35 Illinois agility run test results table. Adapted, with permission, from Ross Bull, Robert Davis, Jan Roscoe, Physical Education and the Study of Sport, 2nd ed., copyright Mosby (2000)

p. 35 Lewis Nomogram. Adapted. © Fox, Edward et al. The Psychological Basis of Physical Education and Athletics, 1988, McGraw-Hill. Material is reproduced with permission of the McGraw-Hill Companies.

p. 41 J-P Nomogram. Research Quarterly for Exercise and Sport (RQES), Vol. 52, 380–384

p. 82 Eysenck's Personality Dimensions. Figure is reproduced with permission from The H.J. Eysenck Memorial Fund

p. 83 Profile of Mood States graph. Adapted, with permission, from P. Klavora and J.V. Daniel, Coach, Athlete and the Sport Psychologist (1979)

p. 114 Bone density differences due to playing sport. Adapted, with permission, from the American Society for Bone and Mineral Research (ASBMR).

This book is designed to help you through your BTEC First Sport Award, and is divided into the six units of the qualification.

About your BTEC First in Sport

Choosing to study for a BTEC First Sport qualification is a great decision to make for lots of reasons. More and more people are looking to improve their personal fitness, so there is a growing demand for personal trainers and fitness instructors. There is also an increased interest in professional sport due to the UK hosting the 2012 Olympic Games. The sport sector offers a wide variety of careers. Your BTEC will sharpen your skills for employment or further study.

About the authors

Mark Adams is head of Sport and PE at Loreto Sixth Form College, Manchester, and is also a consultant with the Premier League education learning team. He has been involved in the development of sport qualifications for 12 years.

Adam Gledhill has 12 years' experience teaching in Further and Higher Education, and has been involved with qualification development for a number of years. Alongside teaching, Adam is currently working toward a PhD in Sport Psychology, while also providing Sport Science support to youth athletes in a range of sports.

Pam Phillippo has played a key role in the development of BTEC Sport qualifications and is an expert in psychophysiology. Formerly a lecturer in Further Education and Higher Education, and having worked with GB athletes, her specialist fields include fitness testing and training, exercise prescription, and experimental methods.

This book is designed to help you use your skills and knowledge in work-related situations, and assist you in getting the most from your course.

These introductions give you a snapshot of what to expect from each unit – and what you should be aiming for by the time you finish it.

How this unit is assessed

Learning aims describe what you will be doing in the unit.

A learner shares how working through the unit has helped them.

Features of this book

There are lots of features in this book to help you learn about the topics in each unit, and to have fun along the way!

Topic references show which parts of the BTEC you are covering.

Get started with a short activity or discussion about the topic.

Key terms are important words or phrases that you will come across. Key terms appear in blue bold text and are defined within the topic or in a key terms box on the page. Also see the glossary.

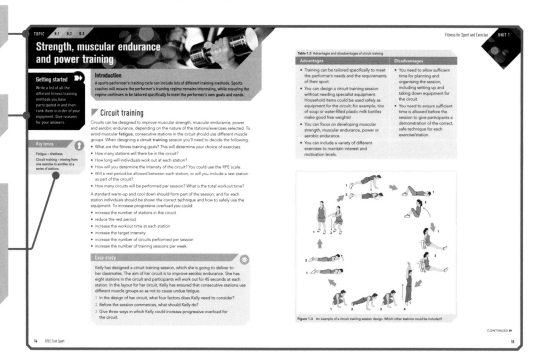

Activity 3.1   Assessing personality

Watch a selection of different sports, pick an athlete to watch in each, and then answer the following questions:

- Which traits and behaviours do they display while they are performing?
- What do these traits/behaviours suggest about their personality type?

Activities will help you learn about the topic. These can be completed in pairs or groups, or sometimes on your own.

Assessment practice 1.1

1 Which component of fitness can have kgm/s as its unit of measurement? Select the correct answer. [1]

A Anaerobic power

B Reaction time

C Speed

D Muscular strength

2 Give three reasons why speed is an important component of physical fitness for basketball players. [3]

A chance to practise answering the types of test questions that you may come across in the onscreen test. (For Unit 1 only.)

Assessment activity 3.3   *English*   2C.P6 | 2C.P7 | 2C.M4 | 2C.D3

You have been asked to prepare a presentation for a group of young athletes to educate them on anxiety, the effects of arousal and the different ways of controlling anxiety. As part of your presentation, you need to include information about:

- different types of anxiety, using relevant examples of each
- the effects of arousal and anxiety on sports performance, using four theories
- imagery and relaxation techniques as methods of controlling arousal and anxiety, and improving sports performance.

Tips

- Give your views on which theories you believe accurately explain the relationship between arousal, anxiety and performance, which you think don't, and why.
- Consider each of the different methods to control arousal – which techniques would be most effective at controlling arousal, and why?

Activities that relate to the unit's assessment critera. These activities will help you prepare for your assignments and contain tips to help you achieve your potential. (For all units **except** Unit 1.)

Just checking

1 What do the initials EPI stand for?

2 Which mood states does the POMS questionnaire measure?

3 What would you look for when conducting behavioural observations?

Use these to check your knowledge and understanding of the topic you have just covered.

Someone who works in the sport industry explains how this unit of the BTEC First applies to the day-to-day work they do as part of their job.

WorkSpace

Samantha

19-year-old football coach

I really like my job. I get to coach football to all different age ranges and abilities, all of which present different challenges.

One of the biggest issues that I face is trying to get people to train outside when it is cold and wet. Trying to get them to concentrate on different areas for improvement is difficult when they just want to keep moving all the time if the weather is bad!

Another issue that I often come across is when players start to worry about the opposition, thinking that they might not be able to beat them because they might have lost to the same opposition before. It is really difficult for me as the coach if players go into a game already having lost in their minds.

One of the biggest benefits of understanding the mind and sports performance is knowing about different ways to motivate my players and different ways of helping them to cope with their performance-related worries.

Think about it

1 Why do you think it is important for sports coaches to have an understanding of the mind and sports performance?

2 How would the information on motivation benefit Samantha in her coaching role?

3 How would the information on arousal, anxiety and performance benefit Samantha in her coaching role?

4 Is this a job that you would be interested in, and if so, why?

101

This section gives you the chance to think more about the role that this person does, and whether you would want to follow in their footsteps once you've completed your BTEC.

BTEC Assessment Zone

You will be assessed in two different ways for your BTEC First in Sport qualification. For most units, your teacher/tutor will set assignments for you to complete. These may take the form of projects where you research, plan, prepare, and evaluate a piece of work or activity. The table in the BTEC Assessment Zone explains what you must do in order to achieve each of the assessment criteria. Each unit of this book contains a number of assessment activities to help you with these assessment criteria.

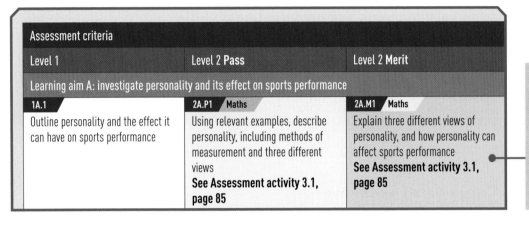

Assessment criteria		
Level 1	Level 2 **Pass**	Level 2 **Merit**
Learning aim A: investigate personality and its effect on sports performance		
1A.1	**2A.P1** Maths	**2A.M1** Maths
Outline personality and the effect it can have on sports performance	Using relevant examples, describe personality, including methods of measurement and three different views **See Assessment activity 3.1, page 85**	Explain three different views of personality, and how personality can affect sports performance **See Assessment activity 3.1, page 85**

The table in the BTEC Assessment Zone explains what you must do in order to achieve each of the assessment criteria, and signposts assessment activities in this book to help you to prepare for your assignments

For Unit 1 of your BTEC, you will be assessed by an onscreen test. The BTEC Assessment Zone for this unit helps you to prepare for your test by showing you some of the different types of questions you may need to answer.

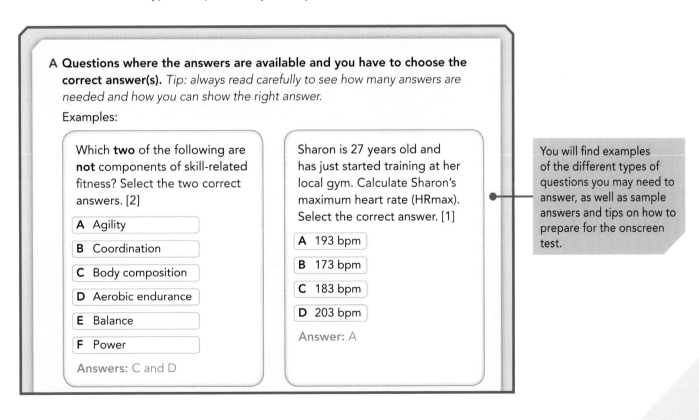

A Questions where the answers are available and you have to choose the correct answer(s). *Tip: always read carefully to see how many answers are needed and how you can show the right answer.*

Examples:

Which **two** of the following are **not** components of skill-related fitness? Select the two correct answers. [2]

A Agility

B Coordination

C Body composition

D Aerobic endurance

E Balance

F Power

Answers: C and D

Sharon is 27 years old and has just started training at her local gym. Calculate Sharon's maximum heart rate (HRmax). Select the correct answer. [1]

A 193 bpm

B 173 bpm

C 183 bpm

D 203 bpm

Answer: A

You will find examples of the different types of questions you may need to answer, as well as sample answers and tips on how to prepare for the onscreen test.

Planning and getting organised

The first step in managing your time is to plan ahead and be well organised. Some people are naturally good at this. They think ahead, write down commitments in a diary or planner and store their notes and handouts neatly and carefully so they can find them quickly.

How good are your working habits?

Improving your planning and organisational skills

1 Use a diary to schedule working times into your weekdays and weekends.

2 Also use the diary to write down exactly what work you have to do. You could use this as a 'to do' list and tick off each task as you go.

3 Divide up long or complex tasks into manageable chunks and put each 'chunk' in your diary with a deadline of its own.

4 Always allow more time than you think you need for a task.

Sources of information

You will need to use research to complete your BTEC First assignments, so it's important to know what sources of information are available to you. These are likely to include the following:

Take it further

If you become distracted by social networking sites or texts when you're working, set yourself a time limit of 10 minutes or so to indulge yourself. You could even use this as a reward for completing a certain amount of work.

Key term

Bias – People often have strong opinions about certain topics. This is called 'bias'. Newspaper or magazine articles, or information found on the internet, may be biased to present a specific point of view.

Remember!

Store relevant information when you find it – keep a folder on your computer specifically for research – so you don't have to worry about finding it again at a later date.

Textbooks
These cover the units of your qualification and provide activities and ideas for further research.

Internet
A vast source of information, but not all sites are accurate and information and opinions can often be **biased** – you should always double-check facts you find online.

Sources of information

Newspapers and magazines
These often cover sport topics in either dedicated sport sections or through articles about sports performers and sports events.

People
People you know can be a great source of opinion and experience – particularly if you want feedback on an idea.

Television
Programmes such as *Soccer AM* and *Match of the Day* can give you an insight into the world of sport. The news also regularly reports on the world of sport.

Organising and selecting information

Organising your information

Once you have used a range of sources of information for research, you will need to organise the information so it's easy to use.

- Make sure your written notes are neat and have a clear heading – it's often useful to date them, too.
- Always keep a note of where the information came from (the title of a book, the title and date of a newspaper or magazine and the web address of a website) and, if relevant, which pages.
- Work out the results of any questionnaires you've used.

Selecting your information

Once you have completed your research, re-read the assignment brief or instructions you were given to remind yourself of the exact wording of the question(s) and divide your information into three groups:

1 Information that is totally relevant.
2 Information that is not as good, but which could come in useful.
3 Information that doesn't match the questions or assignment brief very much, but that you kept because you couldn't find anything better!

Check that there are no obvious gaps in your information against the questions or assignment brief. If there are, make a note of them so that you know exactly what you still have to find.

Presenting your work

Before handing in any assignments, make sure:

- you have addressed each part of the question and that your work is as complete as possible
- all spelling and grammar is correct
- you have referenced all sources of information you used for your research
- all work is your own – otherwise you could be committing **plagiarism**
- you have saved a copy of your work.

Key term

Plagiarism – If you are including other people's views, comments or opinions, or copying a diagram or table from another publication, you must state the source by including the name of the author or publication, or the web address. Failure to do this (when you are really pretending other people's work is your own) is known as plagiarism. Check your school's policy on plagiarism and copying.

Introduction

All sports performers want to be the best they can be. To reach optimal levels requires dedication to training, taking into account all factors that contribute to sports performance.

To perform well, you need good levels of fitness achieved by maintaining good health and adopting the behaviours needed to lead your life to the highest quality. A training cycle can incorporate different fitness training methods, the choice of which will often depend on the performer's sport and their personal training needs.

Fitness testing can be incorporated into the training cycle to determine baseline fitness levels and identify areas needing improvement to help the performer reach their potential and perform better in their sport.

Fitness and exercise for sport is core to your programme of study. This unit links to, and underpins, all other units, and is particularly relevant if you would like to work in sports coaching, elite sport or personal training.

Assessment: You will be assessed using an onscreen test lasting one hour.

Learning aims

In this unit you will:

A know about the components of fitness and the principles of training

B explore different fitness training methods

C investigate fitness testing to determine fitness levels.

I have learned all sorts of things about fitness and exercise training in this unit. I've been able to apply this knowledge in my own training and sports performance, and it's helped to give me clearer training goals, which I know I will achieve.

Temi, *16-year-old gym enthusiast*

Fitness for Sport and Exercise

Components of fitness and their importance for sporting success

Introduction

In this section you will learn about physical fitness and skill-related fitness, and why these are important for success in different sports.

Components of physical fitness

There are six components of physical fitness:

1 **Aerobic endurance** – the ability of the cardiorespiratory system to work efficiently, supplying nutrients and oxygen to working muscles during sustained physical activity.

2 **Muscular endurance** – the ability of the muscular system to work efficiently, in which a muscle can repeatedly contract over a period of time against a light to moderate fixed-resistance load.

3 **Flexibility** – the ability to move all joints fluidly through their complete range of movement.

4 **Speed** – distance divided by the time taken, measured in metres per second (m/s). There are three basic types of speed: accelerative speed (sprints up to 30 metres), pure speed (sprints up to 60 metres) and speed endurance (sprints with a short recovery period in-between).

5 **Muscular strength** – the maximum force that a muscle or muscle group can produce. This is measured in kilograms (kg) or Newtons (N).

6 **Body composition** – the relative ratio of fat mass to fat-free mass (vital organs, muscle, bone) in the body.

Components of skill-related fitness

There are five components of skill-related fitness:

1 **Agility** – the ability to move quickly and precisely or change direction without losing balance or time.

2 **Balance** – the ability to maintain your centre of mass over a base of support. There are two types: **static balance** and **dynamic balance**. For instance, a gymnast would use static balance when performing a handstand on the balance beam and dynamic balance when tumbling during a floor routine.

3 **Coordination** – the ability of parts of the body to work together to move smoothly and accurately.

4 **Power** – the work done in a unit of time. It is calculated in the following way:

$$\text{Power} = \text{Force (kg)} \times \text{Distance (m)} / \text{time (min or s)}.$$

This is expressed as kilogram-metres per minute (kgm/min) or kilogram-metres per second (kgm/s).

5 **Reaction time** – the time taken for a sports performer to respond to a stimulus; for example, the time taken for a footballer to analyse a goal-scoring opportunity and decide to attempt a shot at goal by starting the kicking/heading action.

Which fitness components are important to a cricketer?

A gymnast uses static and dynamic balance. What other components of fitness are important for success?

Why fitness components are important for sporting success

In order to meet the demands of their sport and reach **optimal** levels of performance, a sports performer needs to train specific components of fitness. These will vary from sport to sport and position to position. For example, a basketball player needs aerobic endurance, speed, flexibility, power, muscular endurance and strength in order to move effectively around the court, intercept passes and score baskets. They also need to have great agility and footwork, so they can change direction quickly and respond rapidly to the positions of their opponents.

> **Key term**
>
> Optimal – the best, or most favourable.

Activity 1.1   Fitness for different sports

Work in pairs or small groups.

1 Think about the different sports activities you participate in.

2 Select four different sports and draw a spider diagram showing what components of fitness you think are important for success in each one. Depending on the sports selected, you may also need to consider differences between positions played and how this might impact on your choices.

3 Discuss the reasons for your answers and prepare a short presentation to feed back to the rest of your class.

Assessment practice 1.1

1 **Which component of fitness can have kgm/s as its unit of measurement? Select the correct answer. [1]**

  A **Anaerobic power**

  B **Reaction time**

  C **Speed**

  D **Muscular strength**

2 **Give three reasons why speed is an important component of physical fitness for basketball players. [3]**

Determining exercise intensity

Getting started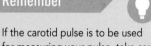

Exercising at the right intensity for you helps you get the most out of your workout. In pairs, discuss how often you work out. How hard do you work during these workouts? Do you think you over work sometimes, or could you push yourself further?

Remember

If the carotid pulse is to be used for measuring your pulse, take care not to apply too much pressure against the carotid artery. This may result in specialised receptors slowing down your heart rate, thereby leading to an invalid resting heart rate result.

Introduction

Exercise intensity is a term used to describe how hard an individual is training; for example the relative speed, rate or level of an individual's exertion. In this topic you will learn about two methods that can be used to determine exercise intensity: heart rate (HR) and Rating of Perceived Exertion (RPE).

Measuring heart rate

Heart rate is measured in beats per minute (bpm), and may indicate an individual's fitness level when taken at rest.

Measuring resting heart rate

At rest, heart rate should preferably be measured via the radial artery in the wrist (rather than the carotid pulse, which is found on either side of your neck).

Sitting down, locate your radial artery by placing your index and middle fingers together on the thumb-side of your opposite wrist; do not use your thumb because it has a light pulse of its own.

Once you find your pulse, ask a friend to start a stopwatch and then count the number of beats you feel for 60 seconds. This is your resting heart rate in beats per minute (bpm).

Measuring radial pulse. Can you measure your resting heart rate (HR)?

Activity 1.2 Measuring heart rate

You'll need a stopwatch for this activity.

1 Measure and record your resting HR.

2 Undertake 15 minutes of light to moderate physical activity. For example, jogging on a treadmill.

3 After 15 minutes of physical activity, sit down immediately and measure your pulse via the radial artery.

4 Record your HR results every minute, until you reach your resting HR.

5 Draw a graph: HR (bpm) against time (seconds or minutes). What do your results suggest about your fitness levels?

6 How long did it take you to reach your original resting HR? How do your results compare to those of your peers? Discuss in small groups.

Measuring exercise heart rate

Training or exercise heart rate can be monitored to ensure you do not push yourself too hard, and to check if you are progressing well with your training regime.

The easiest, most convenient and most accurate way to measure exercise heart rate is to use a heart rate monitor. These are used by professional and amateur sports performers and athletes alike. Athletes and sports performers calculate their **heart rate training zone** to check that they are exercising at the right level of intensity.

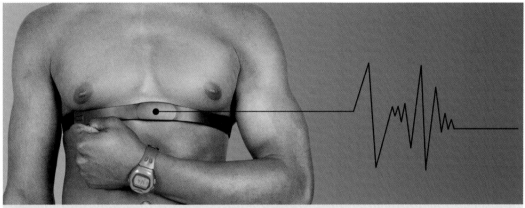

Why not train using a heart rate monitor: what will your results show?

Calculating heart rate training zones

To work out your heart rate training zone, first calculate your maximum heart rate (HRmax):

$$HRmax = 220 - age \text{ (years)}.$$

Next, work out 60% of your HRmax ($0.6 \times$ HRmax), which is the lower heart rate training zone. Finally, work out 85% of your HRmax ($0.85 \times$ HRmax), which is the upper heart rate training zone. The range between these two numbers is the recommended training zone for cardiovascular health and fitness. You'll need plenty of practice at measuring resting heart rate, exercise heart rate and calculating training zones.

Worked example

A healthy 20-year-old would work out their heart rate training zone using the following calculations:

- HRmax: $220 - 20 = 200$ bpm
- lower heart rate training zone: $0.6 \times 200 = 120$ bpm

- upper heart rate training zone: $0.85 \times 200 = 170$ bpm.

Therefore, a healthy 20-year-old has a recommended exercise heart rate of between 120 bpm and 170 bpm.

Assessment practice 1.2

Malcolm is 30 years old and Vivienne is 48 years old.

1 Calculate their maximum heart rates. (4)	2 Calculate their lower and upper heart rate training zones for cardiovascular health and fitness. (4)

CONTINUED ▶▶

Using the RPE scale as a measure of exercise intensity

Another way of determining exercise intensity is to use the Rating of Perceived Exertion (RPE) scale, developed by Professor Gunnar Borg in 1970. The scale can be used to rate an individual's level of physical exertion during physical activity or exercise.

The scale starts at 6 and goes up to 20, where 6 means 'no exertion at all' (at rest) and 20 is 'maximal exertion' (for example, the feeling you have as you make an all out effort for the finish line of a sprint race). You will see in Figure 1.1 that some of the numbers are represented by verbal cues.

Plenty of practice is needed to learn how to use the scale properly. When giving a rating, the individual needs to take into account all sensations of physical stress, effort and fatigue that they are feeling. This will include strain and fatigue in exercising muscles, and feelings of breathlessness.

Rating of Perceived Exertion	Intensity
6	No exertion at all
7	Extremely light
8	
9	Very light
10	
11	
12	
13	Somewhat hard
14	
15	Hard (heavy)
16	
17	Very hard
18	
19	Extremely hard
20	Maximal exertion

Figure 1.1 The Borg (1970) 6–20 RPE scale

Relationship between RPE and HR

Instead of using a HR monitor, you can use the RPE scale to predict the exercise HR of an individual using the relationship:

$$RPE \times 10 = HR \text{ (bpm)}$$

Worked example

If an individual gives a rating of '15 Hard (heavy)', they can predict their exercise HR by using the following calculation:

- RPE × 10 = HR (bpm)
- 15 × 10 = 150 bpm

Therefore, the individual's exercise HR will be approximately 150 bpm.

Why not train using a treadmill? What RPE would you achieve?

Activity 1.3　Determining exercise intensity

Work in small groups.

1 Perform a short warm-up.

2 Set up a 30-minute circuit training session for aerobic endurance. One person in each group should be in charge of recording HR data. Everyone else in the group should wear a heart rate monitor and participate in the training session.

3 Work out your HRmax using the equation: 220 − age (years).

4 Next, calculate your HR training zone for cardiovascular health and fitness (60–85% HRmax).

5 Take part in the training circuit. Your HR and RPE will be recorded after you have exercised at each station.

6 On completion of the 30 minutes, analyse HR and RPE data collected. Answer the following questions:

- Did each participant reach their calculated training zone for cardiovascular health and fitness?

- According to their RPE, how difficult/tiring did participants find it training at this level?

- Did participants go above their training zone? If so, what were possible reasons for this?

7 Discuss your results as a group.

Assessment practice 1.3

1 Frida is 33 years old and exercises in the gym. She records her RPE during the following activities:

Exercise	RPE	Heart rate (bpm)
Exercise bike	13	
Free weights	15	
Treadmill	16	

a Complete the table to show Frida's heart rate (bpm) for these three activities. (3)

b Frida wants to work at 70% HRmax. Using the table above, work out which type of exercise would give her this HR training zone? (1)

2 Describe how the Borg RPE Scale can be used to determine exercise intensity. (2)

The principles of training

Introduction

When planning and undertaking training programmes you need to incorporate the basic principles of training.

The basic principles of training (FITT)

The **FITT principle** is:

- **Frequency** – the number of training sessions you complete over a period of time. Aim for three to five sessions per week.
- **Intensity** – how hard you train. Intensity can be prescribed using HR or RPE.
- **Time** – how long you train for. Aim for 15 to 60 minutes of activity, depending on the intensity. If you have low levels of fitness, then reduce intensity and increase time.
- **Type** – how you train. The appropriate method(s) of training should be selected according to your needs and goals. For example, to train for muscular strength, endurance and power, you could do circuit training, or use free weights in the gym.

Additional principles of training

Fitness training programmes are designed and based on the FITT principle and the following additional principles of training, which can be discussed and agreed between performer and coach:

- **Progressive overload** – in order to progress, training needs to be demanding enough to cause your body to adapt, improving performance. Increase your training workload gradually. This can be done by increasing frequency, intensity or time, or by reducing recovery times. But don't use all of these methods at once, as the increase in workload may lead to over training resulting in injury or illness.
- **Specificity** – training should be specific to your preferred sport, activity, or developing physical/skill-related fitness goals.
- **Individual differences/needs** – the programme should be designed to meet your training goals, needs, ability, level of fitness, skill level and exercise likes/dislikes.
- **Adaptation** – this occurs during the recovery period after the training session is complete. Adaptation is how your body increases its ability to cope with training loads.
- **Reversibility** – if you stop training, or the intensity of training is not sufficient to cause adaptation, training effects are reversed. Reversibility is also known as de-training.
- **Variation** – it is important to maintain interest; this helps an individual keep to their training schedule. Vary your training programme to avoid boredom and maintain enjoyment.
- **Rest and recovery** – these are essential to allow the body to repair and adapt, and for the renewal of body tissues. If your body doesn't get a chance to recover then the rate of progression can be reduced.

Training must be specific to the performer's needs. What are your training goals and needs?

WorkSpace

Charlie McLaren

Personal trainer and life coach

I work for a private gym. I am responsible for:

- working with clients to agree training goals and needs
- assessing client fitness to determine baseline levels
- fitness training programme design
- monitoring client progress towards meeting training goals
- contributing to the gym's lifestyle and fitness activities programme.

I love my job, and in this line of work that's really important. It's my role to motivate clients, encourage personal belief and self-confidence, and give them the support needed to achieve their personal training goals.

My main role at the gym is fitness testing and assessment – clients need to know their baseline fitness levels so that clear goals can be agreed. I usually carry out a range of different fitness tests on clients, which cover the different components of fitness, such as skinfold testing for % body fat. Once I have talked clients through their results we can then discuss training goals and move forward with programme design.

Establishing a regular fitness training regime in everyday life can often mean people having to juggle their work and life commitments, but there's always a way to fit training in.

To be successful in this industry you need leadership and coaching skills and qualities, but personality is important too. Being enthusiastic, approachable, honest and confident are all important traits that clients look for in a personal trainer.

Think about it

1 What areas have you covered in this unit that provide you with knowledge and skills used by a personal trainer and lifestyle coach?

2 What further skills might you need to develop if you were to become a personal trainer?

3 Think about how you would measure clients' heart rates to aid training programme design.

Flexibility training

Getting started

People have different levels of flexibility. Ask the teacher to provide a sit and reach box and, as a group, do the sit and reach test. Record your results. Some of the class may be able to reach further than others. Afterwards, discuss why this might be and how you could improve your flexibility.

Key terms

Flexibility – having an adequate range of motion in all joints of the body.

Isometric – muscular action in which tension develops, but there is no change in muscle length and no joint movement. For example, when doing a side plank.

What type of stretch is this athlete performing?

Introduction

Flexibility is important for all sports performers, whether you are a 110 metres hurdler stretching to clear the hurdle, a footballer extending for the ball or a tennis player reaching to take a forehand. There are three types of flexibility fitness training methods: **static stretching**, **ballistic stretching** and the **Proprioceptive Neuromuscular Facilitation (PNF)** technique.

Static stretching

Static stretching involves slowly stretching a muscle to the limit of its range of movement and then holding the stretch still for 10 to 20 seconds. It is usually used as part of a standard warm-up routine, to help warm muscles and joints ready for exercise. There are two types of static flexibility training:

- **Active stretching** – stretches are performed by a sports performer on their own. The performer applies force to stretch and lengthen the muscles.
- **Passive stretching** – this is also known as assisted stretching and requires the help of another person or an object, such as a chair or wall. The other person (or object) applies an external force, causing the muscle to stretch.

Ballistic stretching

Ballistic stretching involves making fast, jerky movements, usually in the form of bouncing or bobbing through the full range of movement. This form of stretching can incorporate sport-specific movements that take a joint past its normal range of movement. Ballistic stretching must be performed with care, as incorrect technique can lead to muscle soreness and injury.

Proprioceptive Neuromuscular Facilitation (PNF) technique

This is an advanced form of passive stretching, which is often used in rehabilitation programmes. The PNF technique inhibits the stretch reflex, which occurs when a muscle is stretched to its full capability, so that an even greater range of movement can occur. When performing PNF, remember to listen to your body – pain signals will tell you if you have taken the stretch too far. PNF must be performed carefully with a partner. There are three phases:

1 Stretch the muscle to the upper limit of its range of movement.

2 With the help of your partner, contract the muscle **isometrically** for 6–10 seconds.

3 Relax the muscle, and then with the help of your partner perform a static (passive) stretch enabling an even greater stretch to be achieved.

Table 1.1 Advantages and disadvantages of the PNF technique

Advantages	Disadvantages
• Flexibility training can be made sport-specific • Little cost involved, no need for specialist equipment • Improved flexibility may help to reduce injuries	• Need to be experienced to perform PNF training safely • May require two individuals working together to perform the technique

Activity 1.4 Limbering up

Work in small groups.

1 Look at Figure 1.2. For each labelled area of the body, each group member needs to practically demonstrate a different active stretch, which should be held for approximately 10 seconds.

2 Once you have demonstrated a stretch, the person next to you has to demonstrate your stretch and also select their own stretch for a different part of the body, and so on. Repeat in your group until all labelled parts of the body have been covered.

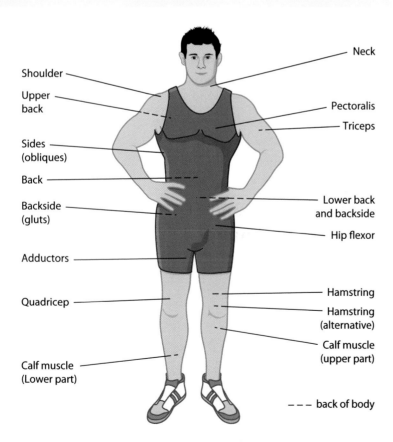

Figure 1.2 Major muscles of the body

Strength, muscular endurance and power training

Key terms

Fatigue – tiredness.

Circuit training – moving from one exercise to another at a series of stations.

Introduction

A sports performer's training cycle can include lots of different training methods. Sports coaches will ensure the performer's training regime remains interesting, while ensuring the regime continues to be tailored specifically to meet the performer's own goals and needs.

Circuit training

Circuits can be designed to improve muscular strength, muscular endurance, power and aerobic endurance, depending on the nature of the stations/exercises selected. To avoid muscular **fatigue**, consecutive stations in the circuit should use different muscle groups. When designing a **circuit training** session you'll need to decide the following:

- What are the fitness training goals? This will determine your choice of exercises.
- How many stations will there be in the circuit?
- How long will individuals work out at each station?
- How will you determine the intensity of the circuit? You could use the RPE scale.
- Will a rest period be allowed between each station, or will you include a rest station as part of the circuit?
- How many circuits will be performed per session? What is the total workout time?

A standard warm-up and cool down should form part of the session, and for each station individuals should be shown the correct technique and how to safely use the equipment. To increase progressive overload you could:

- increase the number of stations in the circuit
- reduce the rest period
- increase the workout time at each station
- increase the target intensity
- increase the number of circuits performed per session
- increase the number of training sessions per week.

Case study

Kelly has designed a circuit training session, which she is going to deliver to her classmates. The aim of her circuit is to improve aerobic endurance. She has eight stations in the circuit and participants will work out for 45 seconds at each station. In the layout for her circuit, Kelly has ensured that consecutive stations use different muscle groups so as not to cause undue fatigue.

1 In the design of her circuit, what four factors does Kelly need to consider?
2 Before the session commences, what should Kelly do?
3 Give three ways in which Kelly could increase progressive overload for the circuit.

Table 1.2 Advantages and disadvantages of circuit training

Advantages	Disadvantages
• Training can be tailored specifically to meet the performer's needs and the requirements of their sport. • You can design a circuit training session without needing specialist equipment. Household items could be used safely as equipment for the circuit; for example, tins of soup or water-filled plastic milk bottles make good free weights! • You can focus on developing muscular strength, muscular endurance, power or aerobic endurance. • You can include a variety of different exercises to maintain interest and motivation levels.	• You need to allow sufficient time for planning and organising the session, including setting up and taking down equipment for the circuit. • You need to ensure sufficient time is allowed before the session to give participants a demonstration of the correct, safe technique for each exercise/station.

Figure 1.3 An example of a circuit training session design. Which other stations could be included?

CONTINUED ▶▶

Free weights

Barbells or dumb-bells are types of free weights and can be used to perform a range of **constant-resistance exercises**. Examples of exercises include: bicep curls, tricep extensions, upright rows, squats, bent-over rows, seated overhead presses, lateral raises, front raises and bench presses.

There is a greater chance of injury when using **free weights** as opposed to **fixed-resistance machines**, and care must be taken to ensure correct, safe technique and use of equipment. When using heavy weights, the use of a **spotter** is recommended. A standard warm-up and cool down should form part of the session.

Weight training tips

- **Warm-up** – a good warm-up and range of stretches before you start training will help prepare your joints for movement and help avoid injury.
- **Body alignment** – if standing, feet should be shoulder-width apart with knees slightly bent. As the weight is lifted, movement should be slow and controlled.
- **Breathing technique** – do not hold your breath as this can increase blood pressure and could cause a heart attack. Breathe out as the weight is lifted.
- **Intensity** – do not use weights that are so heavy that they can't be lifted at least six times. Heavy resistance can be damaging to skeletal and joint structures. Intensity can be determined by using the percentage of an individual's **repetition maximum** (% 1–RM).
- **Number of sets** – every set should consist of 8 to 12 repetitions (reps). As training progresses, overload can be achieved by increasing the number of repetitions in a set (up to 20), and then by increasing the weight and dropping the reps back to 8.
- **Training for maximum strength** – use low reps and heavier weights (90% 1–RM and 6 reps).
- **Training for strength endurance** – use high reps and lighter weights (50% to 60% 1–RM and 20 reps).
- **Training for elastic strength** – use medium reps and weights (75% 1–RM and 12 reps).
- **Number of exercises** – include one to two sets of six different exercises in each workout. Training should cover all the major muscle groups.
- **Order of exercises** – focus on core exercises before assistance exercises; alternate between upper and lower body and push and pull exercises.
- **After training** – perform a cool down and developmental stretching (where stretches are held for 15–20 seconds). This will help to reduce muscle soreness, prevent cramps and increase joint range of movement.

Individual using free weights

Key terms

Constant-resistance exercises – where the amount of resistance for a muscle/muscle group remains the same throughout the repetition.

Free weights – a weight that is not attached to another machine or device.

Fixed-resistance machines – weight training equipment, made up of a stack of weights and pulley system, where a weight or fixed amount of resistance is used.

Spotter – a person who watches and helps a participant during a particular weight training exercise by knowing when to intervene in order to prevent injury to the participant.

Repetition maximum – 1–RM is the maximal force that can be exerted by a muscle or muscle group in a single contraction.

Table 1.3 Advantages and disadvantages of training with free weights

Advantages	Disadvantages
• Training can be sport-specific, targeting specific muscles and muscle groups • Effective method for strength and endurance gains	• Session needs careful organisation, ensuring use of correct, safe technique • May need access to a gym or leisure/sports centre for full range of equipment • The equipment needed can be expensive • May need a spotter

◤ Plyometrics

Plyometrics training develops sport-specific explosive power and strength and is used widely in sports such as track athletics, netball, basketball and volleyball.

Plyometrics training involves exercises in which muscles are quickly and repeatedly stretched/lengthened and then contracted/shortened, thus producing great force.

Plyometrics drills, such as skipping, arm swings and jogging drills, performed at **submaximal** levels, are usually used as a warm-up. Low-stress activities are used for cool down, such as light jogging and walking. Plyometrics training must be undertaken with care and should take into account the experience of the person and the level of intensity of the exercises to be performed. This type of training can be physically stressful and cause muscle soreness.

The basic equipment needed to perform plyometrics exercises includes: boxes, benches, hurdles, cones and medicine balls.

Different types of exercises include standing jumps, **incline press-ups**, jumping, bounding, skipping, hopping and medicine ball exercises for core strength.

Plyometrics training is used to increase explosive power and strength.

Key terms

Submaximal – exercising below an individual's maximal level of physical effort.

Incline press-ups – a press-up exercise where the hands are placed on a raised surface, for example, on a bench or chair.

Did you know?

Plyometrics training used to be known as 'jump training'.

Table 1.4 Advantages and disadvantages of plyometrics

Advantages	Disadvantages
• Training can be made sport-specific • Little cost involved; no need for specialist equipment	• Need to be experienced to perform this type of training safely

Aerobic endurance training

Getting started ▶▶

Think about the different sports and physical activities you take part in over the course of a month. What different fitness training methods do you use? Write a list and compare in small groups.

Introduction

In this section you will explore the different fitness training methods that can be used to develop your aerobic endurance.

Continuous training

Continuous training – also known as long, slow, distance or steady-state training – is where performers train at a steady pace and moderate intensity for at least 30 minutes. Because the training intensity is relatively low, it is a useful training method for beginners who may have a lower level of fitness and also for sports performers who are recovering from injury. A standard warm-up and cool down should form part of the session.

Table 1.5 Advantages and disadvantages of continuous training

Advantages	Disadvantages
• No special equipment needed • Easy training method to organise and carry out • Training can be made sport-specific • Good for building an endurance base	• Training for long distances can be monotonous • Higher risk of injury if running on a hard surface • Only develops aerobic endurance, not anaerobic

Fartlek training

The term 'fartlek' refers to a Swedish training method meaning 'speed play'. A standard warm-up and cool down should form part of the session. Training is usually performed outdoors, and is continuous, with no rest. The performer varies the intensity of training by running at different speeds or over different terrains (such as cross-country running or training on a beach). Intensity of training may be increased using equipment, such as running with a harness or a weighted backpack.

Table 1.6 Advantages and disadvantages of fartlek training

Advantages	Disadvantages
• Can be made sport-specific • No need for specialist equipment • The performer can control the intensity level • Adds variety and interest to training	• Need for careful control of training intensity • Performer needs good self-discipline and motivation to maintain work rates

Fartlek training uses a variety of terrains.

Interval training

For this training method the individual alternates work periods with rest or recovery periods. By varying the intensity and length of work periods, training can improve anaerobic and aerobic endurance. Work intervals for aerobic endurance will be approximately 60% **VO$_2$ max**. Typical work time varies from 30 seconds to 5 minutes, and recovery can be jogging or walking or even a complete rest.

A standard warm-up and cool down should form part of the session. For aerobic endurance training, decrease the number of rest periods and decrease work intensity. When planning interval training you need to consider:

- the duration of the work interval
- the duration of the rest interval
- the intensity of the work interval
- the intensity of the rest interval
- the total number of intervals in the training session.

Key term

VO$_2$ max – the maximum amount of oxygen uptake, usually measured in ml of oxygen per kg of body mass per minute. It is a measure of cardiorespiratory endurance.

Table 1.7 Advantages and disadvantages of interval training

Advantages	Disadvantages
• Allows clear progressive overload to be built into training by increasing the number of intervals, increasing intensity of the work periods, increasing the intensity of the rest period, or decreasing the duration of the rest period • Can be tailored to specific sports • No special equipment required • Can be used for aerobic and anaerobic endurance • Distance, time and intensity can meet individual training need	• Performer may lose interest due to repetition • Needs careful planning

Rest and recovery periods can involve jogging, walking or even complete rest.

Assessment practice 1.4

Rudi has joined his local gym with the aim of improving his strength and muscular endurance.

1 Which fitness training method should Rudi follow to help him achieve his aim? (1)

2 Explain why Rudi should increase progressive overload and give an example of how he could do this in circuit training. (2)

3 Rudi wants to train for maximum strength. What % 1–RM and reps should he be working at? (2)

Speed training

Introduction

The following fitness training methods are designed to improve a performer's speed. Speed training can be made sport-specific and often takes the form of drills.

Hollow sprints

This technique involves completing a series of sprints separated by a 'hollow' period of jogging or walking. A standard warm-up and cool down should form part of the session. A typical session could be as follows:

1 Set out ten cones at 20-metre intervals.
2 Sprint for 20 metres, then jog for 20 metres, alternating between the two until you reach the final cone. This is one set.
3 Complete eight sets in total. If intensity is too great, replace 'hollow' jog period with a walk instead.

Table 1.8 Advantages and disadvantages of hollow sprints

Advantages	Disadvantages
• No special equipment needed • Easy training method to organise and carry out • Training can be made sport-specific	• Performer may lose interest due to repetition • Need to maintain focus and motivation throughout

Acceleration sprints

For this type of training the pace is gradually increased from a standing or rolling start to jogging, then to striding and a maximum sprint. A standard warm-up and cool down should be carried out. Different drills can be used, such as resistance drills and hill sprints. Rest intervals of jogging or walking are used in-between each repetition. For example, an acceleration hill workout involves:

1 25-metre hills (at 15-degree gradient) × 8 repetitions
2 Walk or jog back down the hill to the start
3 1.5 to 2.5 minute rest between each repetition.

Table 1.9 Advantages and disadvantages of acceleration sprints

Advantages	Disadvantages
• No special equipment needed • Easy training method to organise and carry out	• Performer may lose interest due to repetition • Need to maintain focus and motivation throughout

Interval training

Interval training involves the individual alternating work periods with rest and recovery periods. For speed training, the work intervals are shorter and more intense, where the individual will work at a high intensity, close to their maximum possible level of physical effort.

A standard warm-up and cool down should form part of the session.

When designing an interval training session to develop speed, increase the number of rest periods, decrease the work interval and increase the work intensity.

Table 1.10 Advantages and disadvantages of interval training

Advantages	Disadvantages
• No special equipment required • Can be tailored to specific sports • Can be tailored specifically for speed and anaerobic endurance gains • Distance, time and intensity can meet individual training needs	• Performer may lose interest due to repetition • Needs careful planning

Performers undertaking sprint drills. What type of training session could you design?

Activity 1.5 Designing a training programme

1 Plan and design your own six-week training programme specific to your own personal goals and needs.
You'll need to show how you have:
- incorporated the principles of training into your design
- included details of why you have selected the particular training methods.

2 Maintain a training diary to show how you have:
- applied exercise intensity and principles of training to your selected fitness training method(s)
- applied fitness training method(s) to your own needs/goals/aims/objectives.

 Link

This activity could be carried out alongside *Unit 5: Training for Personal Fitness*, giving you the opportunity to implement the programme you have designed.

Fitness testing

Getting started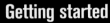

Fitness testing is used in sport to gain information about the athlete's physical- and skill-related ability. Think about the fitness tests you have done in school, e.g. the bleep test. In pairs, discuss why you think fitness testing is important for athletes and what you learnt from your own fitness test results.

Introduction

In this topic you will learn about the requirements for fitness test administration and the procedures that need to be carried out before testing begins.

Why are fitness tests important?

Fitness tests are important because they:

- Provide a coach with baseline data results, which they can compare to normative published data in order to draw conclusions about an individual's fitness level.
- Give a starting point on which to base training programme design. Once training commences, fitness tests can then be used during the training cycle to show the progress of a training regime and its success so far.
- Can give a sports performer or athlete clear goals and targets to aim for. Appropriate recommendations for fitness improvements can be made according to the individual's test results and specific training needs.

Did you know? ❓

Aside from sport, fitness testing is also widely used by the armed forces in their initial fitness assessment for potential recruits and also their ongoing assessment of an individual's fitness throughout their career.

An athlete performing the press-up test. How will you perform?

Pre-test procedures

Gaining informed consent

Before administering or participating in fitness tests the participant should complete an informed consent form. This is documented evidence that shows that the participant has been provided with all the necessary information to undertake each fitness test. Informed consent forms cover the following key points, which confirm that the participant:

- is able to follow the test method
- knows exactly what is required of them during testing
- has fully consented to participation in the fitness tests
- knows that they are able to ask the tester/teacher/assessor any questions relating to the tests
- understands that they can withdraw their consent at any time.

Remember

Each consent form should be signed and dated by the participant, supported by a witness (usually your teacher/assessor) and if participants are under 18 years of age their parent/guardian will also be required to give their informed consent. An example of an informed consent form is shown in Figure 1.4.

Activity 1.6 Designing informed consent forms

Work in pairs or small groups.

1 Design your own informed consent forms for the different fitness tests to be undertaken.

2 You may design one consent form to cover all fitness tests listed in the unit content, or you may design different consent forms with fitness tests grouped under the relevant component of fitness.

Calibration of equipment

Calibration of equipment is the process of checking (and if necessary adjusting) the accuracy of fitness testing equipment before it is used, by comparing it to a recognised standard.

Prior to testing, equipment should be checked carefully. If equipment isn't correctly calibrated it could lead to inaccurate (invalid) results.

INFORMED CONSENT FOR THE MULTISTAGE FITNESS TEST

1. The purpose of the test is to predict an individual's maximal oxygen uptake (aerobic endurance) (VO_2 max in ml/kg/min)
2. This will be determined using the Multistage fitness test. The test will be carried out in the school/college sports hall
3. The participant will carry out standard warming-up and cool down procedures for the test
4. The participant will be required to run between two cones placed 20 metres apart to the 'bleeps' dictated by the audiotape
5. The test is progressive and maximal i.e. the participant is required to continue running until maximal exhaustion or until they are no longer able to keep up with the bleeps
6. All participants will receive method details in full
7. The tester/tutor/assessor is available to answer any relevant queries which may arise concerning the test
8. The participant is free to withdraw consent and discontinue participation in the test at any time
9. Only the tester/tutor/assessor and participant will have access to data recorded from the test which will be stored securely. Participant confidentiality is assured.

I fully understand the scope of my involvement in this fitness test and have freely consented to my participation.

I _____(insert participant name),_____ , understand that my parents/guardian have given permission for me to take part in this fitness test, which will be supervised by _____(insert tutor/assessor name)_____ . I am participating in this fitness test because I want to, and I have been informed that I can discontinue participation without any issues arising.

Participant signature: _____ Date: _____

Tester/tutor/assessor signature: _____ Date: _____

Figure 1.4 Example of an informed consent form

CONTINUED ▶▶

Make sure to record all fitness test results as you get them, so you don't forget.

Accurate measurement and recording of test results

- Allow sufficient time to practise each fitness test method before you begin collecting data. This will increase the likelihood of your results being accurate and reliable.
- Use an appropriate data collection sheet to record your results.
- Record each result as you get it, so you don't forget.
- For reliable results, all fitness tests should be repeated. In a **submaximal fitness test** it may be repeated on the same day (i.e. half-day test–retest). For a **maximal fitness test**, a longer recovery period is required between trials, so a separate day test–retest would be appropriate.
- Use the correct units of measurement. Some fitness tests will require the use of tables or **nomograms** (special charts) to process data and obtain the correct units of measurement for interpretation of test results.
- You will need to use published **normative data tables** to interpret fitness test results.

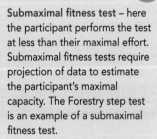

Key terms

Submaximal fitness test – here the participant performs the test at less than their maximal effort. Submaximal fitness tests require projection of data to estimate the participant's maximal capacity. The Forestry step test is an example of a submaximal fitness test.

Maximal fitness test – this requires the participant to make an 'all-out' maximal effort with results recorded at the all-out effort stage. The multistage fitness test is an example of a maximal test.

Reliability, validity and practicality of fitness test methods

By gaining direct experience through undertaking and administering different fitness tests, you will gain an understanding of factors which could affect test reliability and validity.

- **Reliability** is repeatability – the fitness test results obtained should be consistent. If you were to carry out the same fitness test method again, using exactly the same conditions and environment, you should expect the same results.
- **Validity** is the accuracy of the fitness test results, i.e. whether the results you have recorded are a true reflection of what you were actually trying to measure.
- **Practicality** is about how easy it is to carry out the test in terms of the costs involved, time available and equipment requirements. For example, can large groups be tested at once (good practicality) or do participants have to be tested individually because of a lack of resources (poor practicality)?

Advantages and disadvantages of fitness test methods

You'll need to be aware of the advantages and disadvantages of different fitness tests and how these might impact on test selection and administration. Therefore, try to gain first-hand experience by participating in the tests yourself.

Table 1.11 Advantages and disadvantages of fitness test methods

Fitness test	Advantages	Disadvantages
Sit and reach test	• Easy to complete – you can use a bench and ruler if a sit and reach box is unavailable • Quick to administer • Published tables of norms available • Modified tests exist which take into account the distance between the end of the fingers and the sit and reach box	• The test may not be valid for all populations. Research by Jackson and Baker (1986) found that the sit and reach test does not assess lower back flexibility in teenage girls • There are different, inconsistent test methods. For example, some methods include a warm-up, others do not
Multistage fitness test	• Minimal cost involved • Large numbers of participants can be tested at once • Gives good predictions of aerobic endurance provided that participants run until maximal exhaustion	• Reliability and validity of the test depends on the correct technique being used; participants need to run and turn in time with the bleeps. • Not suitable for certain populations, e.g. the elderly • Well-motivated participants needed – for results to be valid, participants must only drop out when they can no longer physically continue • Favours sports performers who make endurance demands of the leg muscle groups (e.g. cyclists and runners)
Illinois agility run test	• Minimal cost involved • Simple test method to administer; no specialist equipment required • Valid test for games players	• Different surfaces can affect times recorded • Risk of slipping depending on choice of surface • Inconsistencies with times recorded • Test cannot distinguish between left and right turning ability • Need to ensure standard layout is used for valid test interpretation against normative published data tables

Activity 1.7   Advantages and disadvantages of the step test

This activity is best completed after you have gained direct experience with the step test method. Work in small groups. In your group, discuss the step test you have participated in and produce a list of the advantages and disadvantages. Where appropriate, give reasons for your answers.

Link

See *Topic C1* for information on how to administer the forestry step test.

Assessment practice 1.5

1 Give two reasons why fitness testing is important. (2)

2 With reference to fitness testing, which term is defined as 'the consistency' of fitness test results? (1)

    A Practicality

    B Reliability

    C Validity

    D Responsibility

Fitness testing methods and results

TOPIC   C.1   C.2   C.3   C.4

Getting started

Ask your teacher for a grip dynamometer. In pairs, take the grip dynamometer test and record your results. What did you think about your result? Did you think it was higher or lower that you thought it would be? Discuss which types of sports would require athletes to have a high grip dynamometer test result and why.

Key term

Published normative data tables – tables used to interpret fitness test results (for example, according to age and gender), in order to provide information about the fitness characteristics of an individual.

Introduction

In this section you will learn 12 different fitness tests. You will need to know the standard test methods, equipment and resources required, the purpose of each test, and how to accurately measure and record test results. You will need to use published normative data tables to interpret fitness test results. We'll look at each test method in turn.

 ## Sit and reach test (flexibility)

This test is used to measure trunk forward flexion, hamstring, hip and lower back range of motion. You will need a standard sit and reach box.

Method

1 Perform a short warm-up prior to this test. Remove your shoes.
2 Sit with your heels placed against the edge of the sit and reach box. Keep your legs flat on the floor, i.e. keep your knees down.
3 Place one hand on top of the other and reach forward slowly. Your fingertips should be in contact with the measuring portion of the sit and reach box. As you reach forward, drop your head between your arms and breathe out as you push forward. Don't use fast, jerky movements, as this may increase risk of injury.
4 The best of three trials should be recorded.

Interpreting results

Use Table 1.12 to interpret your results.

Table 1.12 Sit and reach test results

Rating	Males (cm)	Females (cm)
Excellent	25+	20+
Very good	17	17
Good	15	16
Average	14	15
Poor	13	14
Very poor	9	10

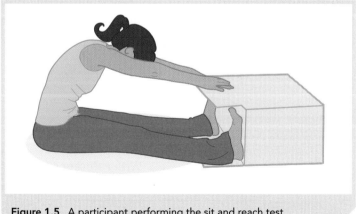

Figure 1.5 A participant performing the sit and reach test.

Grip dynamometer test (strength)

This test is used to measure static strength of the power grip-squeezing muscles, where the whole hand is used as a vice or clamp.

What you will need

Grip dynamometer – a grip dynamometer is a spring device. As force is applied, the spring is compressed and this moves the dynamometer needle, which indicates the result. Digital dynamometers are also available.

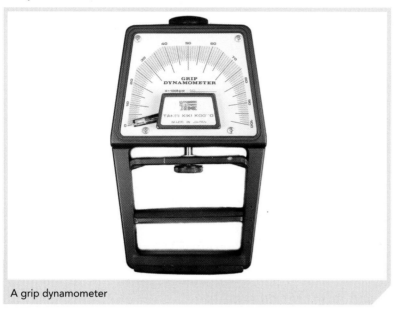

A grip dynamometer

Method

1 Adjust the handgrip size, so the dynamometer feels comfortable to hold.
2 Stand up, with your arms by the side of your body.
3 Hold the dynamometer parallel to the side of your body, with the dial/display facing away from you.
4 Squeeze as hard as possible for 5 seconds, without moving your arm.
5 Carry out three trials on each hand, with a 1 minute rest between trials.

Interpreting results

Use Table 1.13 to interpret your results.

Table 1.13 Grip strength results

Rating	Males aged 15–19 years (kgw)	Females aged 15–19 years (kgw)
Excellent	>52	>32
Good	47–51	28–31
Average	44–46	25–27
Below average	39–43	20–24
Poor	<39	<20

CONTINUED ▶▶

◤ Multistage fitness test (aerobic endurance)

This test is used to predict maximum oxygen uptake (aerobic fitness) levels. The test should be conducted indoors, usually in a sports hall using two lines (or cones) placed 20m apart.

What you will need

- Access to an indoor sports hall
- Cones
- Test audiotape (pre-recording)

Method

1 Perform a short warm-up. Then line up on the start line and on hearing the triple bleep run to the other line, 20m away. You must reach the other line before or on the single bleep that determines each shuttle run.

2 Make sure you turn to run to the other line on the next bleep.

3 You will find that the bleeps get closer and closer together, so you'll need to continually increase your pace.

4 A spotter is used to check that you have reached each line in time with the bleep. If not, you will receive two verbal warnings before being asked to pull out of the test.

5 Continue running until you are physically exhausted, i.e. you have reached maximum exhaustion, at which point your level and shuttle reached are recorded.

Processing and interpreting results

Use Table 1.16 to predict your maximum oxygen consumption (ml/kg/min) and Tables 1.14 and 1.15 to compare your results.

Did you know? ❓

VO$_2$ max, your maximum oxygen uptake, is predicted or measured in millilitres of oxygen per kilogram of body mass per minute (ml/kg/min).

Table 1.14 Aerobic endurance results

Rating	Males aged 15–19 years (ml/kg/min)	Females aged 15–19 years (ml/kg/min)
Excellent	>60	>54
Good	48–59	43–53
Average	39–47	35–42
Below average	30–38	28–34
Poor	<30	<28

Table 1.15 How do your aerobic endurance test results compare to those of elite performers?

Rating	Males aged 18–22 years (ml/kg/min)	Females aged 18–22 years (ml/kg/min)
World-class	>80	>70
Elite	70	63
Trained	57	53
Active	50	43
Untrained	45	39

Table 1.16 Predicted maximum oxygen uptake values (ml/kg/min)

Level	Shuttle	VO_2 max	Level	Shuttle	VO_2 max	Level	Shuttle	VO_2 max	Level	Shuttle	VO_2 max
4	2	26.8	10	2	47.4	15	2	64.6	19	6	79.2
4	4	27.6	10	4	48.0	15	4	65.1	19	8	79.7
4	6	28.3	10	6	48.7	15	6	65.6	19	10	80.2
4	9	29.5	10	8	49.3	15	8	66.2	19	12	80.6
5	2	30.2	10	11	50.2	15	10	66.7	19	15	81.3
5	4	31.0	11	2	50.8	15	13	67.5	20	2	81.8
5	6	31.8	11	4	51.4	16	2	68.0	20	4	82.2
5	9	32.9	11	6	51.9	16	4	68.5	20	6	82.6
6	2	33.6	11	8	52.5	16	6	69.0	20	8	83.0
6	4	34.3	11	10	53.1	16	8	69.5	20	10	83.5
6	6	35.0	11	12	53.7	16	10	69.9	20	12	83.9
6	8	35.7	12	2	54.3	16	12	70.5	20	14	84.3
6	10	36.4	12	4	54.8	16	14	70.9	20	16	84.8
7	2	37.1	12	6	55.4	17	2	71.4	21	2	85.2
7	4	37.8	12	8	56.0	17	4	71.9	21	4	85.6
7	6	38.5	12	10	56.5	17	6	72.4	21	6	86.1
7	8	39.2	12	12	57.1	17	8	72.9	21	8	86.5
7	10	39.9	13	2	57.6	17	10	73.4	21	10	86.9
8	2	40.5	13	4	58.2	17	12	73.9	21	12	87.4
8	4	41.1	13	6	58.7	17	14	74.4	21	14	87.8
8	6	41.8	13	8	59.3	18	2	74.8	21	16	88.2
8	8	42.4	13	10	59.8	18	4	75.3	–	–	–
8	11	43.3	13	13	60.6	18	6	75.8	–	–	–
9	2	43.9	14	2	61.1	18	8	76.2	–	–	–
9	4	44.5	14	4	61.7	18	10	76.7	–	–	–
9	6	45.2	14	6	62.2	18	12	77.2	–	–	–
9	8	45.8	14	8	62.7	18	15	77.9	–	–	–
9	11	46.8	14	10	63.2	19	2	78.3	–	–	–
			14	13	64.0	19	4	78.8	–	–	–

CONTINUED ▶▶

3 cm

Figure 1.6 A participant performing the forestry step test.

Forestry step test (aerobic endurance)

This test is used to predict maximum oxygen uptake (aerobic fitness) levels. The test was developed in 1977 by Brian Sharkey, and is a modified version of the Harvard step test. It is widely used in fitness selection procedures (e.g. for the police force).

A different bench height is used for males and females. For males, the height of the bench should be 40cm, for females, 33cm. The stepping rate of 22.5 steps per minute is the same for both males and females, which means the metronome should be set at a cadence of 90bpm.

What you will need

- Bench
- Metronome
- Stopwatch

Method

1 Stand directly facing the bench and start stepping in time with the beat of the metronome. As soon as you start stepping, the helper should start the stopwatch.

2 Keep to the beat of the metronome, putting one foot onto the bench, then your other foot, then lowering the first foot to the floor, then your other foot – i.e. up, up, down, down.

3 Straighten your legs when you fully step up onto the bench.

4 Keep stepping for 5 minutes, at which point your helper will stop the metronome and you will need to sit down immediately and locate your radial pulse.

5 After 5 minutes and 15 seconds (15 seconds after you have sat down) you will need to count your pulse for 15 seconds (stopping at 5 minutes and 30 seconds).

6 Record your 15-second pulse rate and perform a short cool down.

Processing and interpreting results

Use Tables 1.17a–d to obtain your non-adjusted aerobic fitness level.

- See Table 1.17a or 1.17b (depending on your gender): locate your 15-second pulse in the 'Pulse count' column and find the closest value to your body weight (kg). Where these two values intersect is your non-adjusted aerobic fitness level (ml/kg/min).

- See Table 1.17c: adjust your fitness level to take into account your age, which will provide a more accurate prediction of your aerobic endurance. Locate your closest age in years (left-hand column) and locate your non-adjusted aerobic fitness value (fitness score) along the top. Where these two values intersect is your age-adjusted fitness level (ml/kg/min).

- See Table 1.17d: interpret your aerobic fitness level.

Did you know? ?

Having a high VO_2 max means that your body has a fantastic ability to use oxygen, and is very efficient in extracting oxygen from the air and getting it quickly into the bloodstream and to your working muscles. A high VO_2 max means your muscles have a high capacity to work aerobically over extended periods of time, which is an advantage for endurance-based sports and activities.

Table 1.17a Forestry non-adjusted aerobic fitness values (ml/kg/min) for males

Pulse count	Maximal oxygen consumption (VO$_2$ max)												
45	33	33	33	33	33	32	32	32	32	32	32	32	32
44	34	34	34	34	33	33	33	33	33	33	33	33	33
43	35	35	35	34	34	34	34	34	34	34	34	34	34
42	36	35	35	35	35	35	35	35	35	35	35	34	34
41	36	36	36	36	36	36	36	36	36	36	36	35	35
40	37	37	37	37	37	37	37	37	35	35	35	35	35
39	38	38	38	38	38	38	38	38	38	38	38	37	37
38	39	39	39	39	39	39	39	39	39	39	39	38	38
37	41	40	40	40	40	40	40	40	40	40	40	39	39
36	42	42	41	41	41	41	41	41	41	41	41	40	40
35	43	43	42	42	42	42	42	42	42	42	42	42	41
34	44	44	43	43	43	43	43	43	43	43	43	43	43
33	46	45	45	45	45	45	44	44	44	44	44	44	44
32	47	47	46	46	46	46	46	46	46	46	46	46	46
31	48	48	48	47	47	47	47	47	47	47	47	47	47
30	50	49	49	49	48	48	48	48	48	48	48	48	48
29	52	51	51	51	50	50	50	50	50	50	50	50	50
28	53	53	53	53	52	52	52	52	51	51	51	51	51
27	55	55	55	54	54	54	54	54	54	53	53	53	52
26	57	57	56	56	56	56	56	56	56	55	55	54	54
25	59	59	58	58	58	58	58	58	58	56	56	55	55
24	60	60	60	60	60	60	60	59	59	58	58	57	
23	62	62	61	61	61	61	61	60	60	60	59		
22	64	64	63	63	63	63	62	62	61	61			
21	66	66	65	65	65	64	64	64	62				
20	68	68	67	67	67	67	66	66	65				
Weight (kg)	**54.5**	**59.1**	**63.6**	**68.2**	**72.7**	**77.3**	**81.8**	**86.4**	**91**	**95.4**	**100**	**104.5**	**109**

CONTINUED ▶▶

Table 1.17b Forestry non-adjusted aerobic fitness values (ml/kg/min) for females

Pulse count	Maximal oxygen consumption (VO$_2$ max)											
45										29	29	29
44								30	30	30	30	30
43							31	31	31	31	31	31
42			32	32	32	32	32	32	32	32	32	32
41			33	33	33	33	33	33	33	33	33	33
40			34	34	34	34	34	34	34	34	34	34
39			35	35	35	35	35	35	35	35	35	35
38			36	36	36	36	36	36	36	36	36	36
37			37	37	37	37	37	37	37	37	37	37
36		37	38	38	38	38	38	38	38	38	38	38
35	38	38	39	39	39	39	39	39	39	39	39	39
34	39	39	40	40	40	40	40	40	40	40	40	40
33	40	40	41	41	41	41	41	41	41	41	41	41
32	41	41	42	42	42	42	42	42	42	42	42	42
31	42	42	43	43	43	43	43	43	43	43	43	43
30	43	43	44	44	44	44	44	44	44	44	44	44
29	44	44	45	45	45	45	45	45	45	45	45	45
28	45	45	46	46	46	47	47	47	47	47	47	47
27	46	46	47	48	48	49	49	49	49	49		
26	47	48	49	50	50	51	51	51	51			
25	49	50	51	52	52	53	53					
24	51	52	53	54	54	55						
23	53	54	55	56	56	57						
Weight (kg)	**36.4**	**40.9**	**45.4**	**50.0**	**54.5**	**59.1**	**63.6**	**68.2**	**72.7**	**77.3**	**81.8**	**86.4**

Table 1.17c Age-adjusted fitness levels

Fitness score		30	31	32	33	34	35	36	37	38	39	40	41	42	43	44	45	46	47	48	49	50
Nearest age	15	32	33	34	35	36	37	38	39	40	41	42	43	44	45	46	47	48	49	50	51	53
	20	31	32	33	34	35	36	37	38	39	40	41	42	43	44	45	46	47	48	49	50	51

(cont.)

Fitness score		51	52	53	54	55	56	57	58	59	60	61	62	63	64	65	66	67	68	69	70	71	72
Nearest age	15	54	55	56	57	58	59	60	61	62	63	64	65	66	67	68	69	70	71	72	74	75	76
	20	52	53	54	55	56	57	58	59	60	61	62	63	64	65	66	67	68	69	70	71	72	73

Table 1.17d Aerobic fitness levels

	Fitness category						
	Superior	Excellent	Very good	Good	Fair	Poor	Very poor
Age and gender	Maximum oxygen consumption (ml/kg/min)						
15-year-old male	57+	56–52	51–47	46–42	41–37	36–32	<32
15-year-old female	54+	53–49	48–44	43–39	38–34	33–29	<29
20-year-old male	56+	55–51	50–46	45–41	40–36	35–31	<31
20-year-old female	53+	52–48	47–43	42–38	37–33	32–28	<28

35-metre sprint test (speed)

This test is used to measure and interpret an individual's speed.

What you will need

- Access to an indoor sports hall
- Stopwatch

Method

1 The test is best performed on an indoor athletics track, or an outdoor track on a day when weather conditions will not affect test results.

2 Perform a warm-up.

3 Three people should time the sprint, using stopwatches capable of measuring to one-tenth of a second.

4 Line up on the start line, in a standing start position.

5 As soon as you start sprinting, the timers will start their stopwatches.

6 Sprint as fast as you can, crossing the 35m line.

7 When you cross the 35m line, the timers should stop their stopwatches.

8 Record your time for the sprint to the closest tenth of a second. Take an average result from the three timers.

9 No more than two to three trials can be performed in one day. Allow at least 3 minutes of recovery time between trials. A third trial should only be performed if the difference in times between your first and second trial is greater than 0.20 seconds.

10 Record the best time from your trials as your 35m sprint result.

11 To prevent muscle soreness, perform a cool down followed by static stretching.

Interpreting results

Use Table 1.18 to interpret your results.

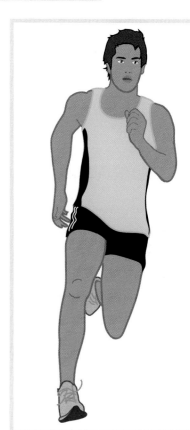

Figure 1.7 A participant performing the 35-metre sprint test.

Table 1.18 35m sprint results

Rating	Males (s)	Females (s)
Excellent	<4.80	<5.30
Good	4.80–5.09	5.30–5.59
Average	5.10–5.29	5.60–5.89
Fair	5.30–5.60	5.90–6.20
Poor	>5.60	>6.20

CONTINUED ▸▸

Did you know? ❓

The Illinois agility run test was originally developed by Dr Thomas Cureton, and later adapted in 1979 by Dr Leroy 'Bud' Getchell who, after a successful career in college baseball and basketball coaching, went on to become a professor of kinesiology and leading researcher and author in the field of fitness and exercise science.

Illinois agility run test (speed and agility)

This test is used to measure an individual's speed and agility, i.e. the ability to move precisely and quickly and change direction without losing balance or time.

The test is performed indoors on a flat non-slip surface, with cones to mark the layout. The length of the course is 10 metres and the width (between start and finishing points) is 5 metres. Four cones mark the start, finish and the two turning points. Four more cones are placed down the centre of the course, 3.3m apart.

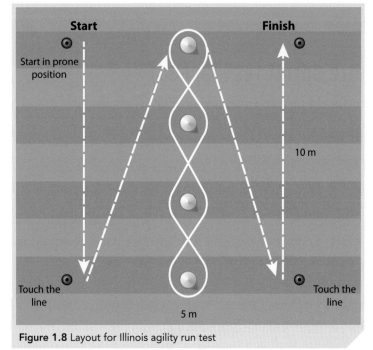

Figure 1.8 Layout for Illinois agility run test

What you will need

- Access to an indoor sports hall
- Cones
- Stopwatch

Method

1 Perform a short warm-up.

2 The starting position for this test is to lie face down, with your elbows flexed and hands placed by the sides of your chest, palms flat on the floor. Your head should be in line with the starting line.

3 On the starter's 'go' command, the stopwatch is started and you must stand up and sprint around the course in the direction indicated, without knocking any of the cones over.

4 Sprint through the finish line; the timing will stop when your chest passes over the finish line.

5 If part of your foot does not touch or go beyond the turning lines or you knock over any cones while navigating the course, you will need to discontinue the test and start again.

6 Complete two trials and interpret your best result (in seconds) using Table 1.19.

Interpreting results

Use Table 1.19 to interpret your results.

Table 1.19 Illinois agility run test results

Results (seconds)					
Gender	Excellent	Above average	Average	Below average	Poor
Male	<15.2	15.2–16.1	16.2–18.1	18.2–19.3	>19.3
Female	<17.0	17.0–17.9	18.0–21.7	21.8–23.0	>23.0

Did you know?

The world record for the Illinois agility run test is held by Australian-rules footballer, Daniel Kerr, who set a time of 11.29 seconds in Melbourne in 2010.

◢ Vertical jump test (anaerobic power)

This test is used to predict the anaerobic power of the quadriceps muscle group.

Key term

Dominant side – an individual may have a dominant/preferred side of the body: i.e. a right-handed individual stands with the right side against the vertical jump board and reaches up with the right hand.

What you will need

- A vertical jump board
- Gymnasts' chalk (if board is not digital)

Method

1 Perform a short warm-up prior to the test.

2 Stand with your **dominant side** against the board, feet together, and reach up as high as you can to record your standing reach height.

3 Only one dip of the arms and knees is permitted. Make the jump and touch the vertical jump board at the peak of your jump.

4 Perform three trials. No rest is required; the time taken to observe and record the height of the jump is all that is needed for recovery between consecutive trials.

Processing and interpreting results

A nomogram is a special chart/diagram that can be used to obtain fitness test results. Use the Lewis nomogram (Figure 1.9) to predict the power of your quadriceps in kgm/s.

- Plot the difference (D) between your standing reach height and your best jump height (cm) on the nomogram line (D).
- Plot your weight in kilograms on the nomogram line (Wt).
- Using a sharpened pencil and ruler, join up the points; the line will cross over the power line (P) to give a prediction of the anaerobic power of your quadriceps muscles (in kgm/s).

Table 1.20 Vertical jump test results

Rating	Males (kgm/s)	Females (kgm/s)
Above average	>105	>90
Average	95	80
Below average	<85	<70

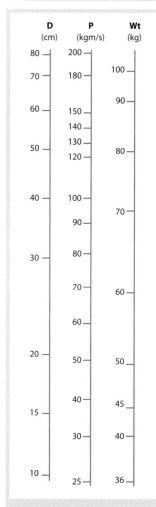

Figure 1.9 Lewis nomogram

CONTINUED ▶▶

One-minute press-up test (muscular endurance)

This test is used to assess the endurance of the muscles of your upper body.

What you will need

- Access to an indoor sports hall
- Exercise mat
- Stopwatch

Method

1 Position yourself on a mat, with your hands shoulder-width apart and arms fully extended.
2 Next, lower your body until your elbows are at 90 degrees.
3 Return to the starting position, with your arms fully extended.
4 Make sure your push-up action is continuous, with no rests in between.
5 Record the total number of press-ups for 1 minute.
6 Due to reduced upper body strength, females may choose to use a modified press-up technique, where in the starting position a bent knee position is assumed.

Interpreting results

Use Table 1.21 or 1.22 to interpret your results.

Table 1.21 One-minute press-up test results (full-body press-ups)

Rating	Males (no. of reps)	Females (no. of reps)
Excellent	>45	>34
Good	35–44	17–33
Average	20–34	6–16
Poor	<19	<5

Table 1.22 One-minute press-up test results (modified press-ups)

Rating	No. of reps
Excellent	>39
Good	34–38
Average	17–33
Fair	6–16
Poor	<6

Activity 1.8 Interpreting fitness test results

Participate in each different fitness test featured in this unit. Then process and interpret your test results:

- Compare your results to normative published data tables. What do your results show?
- Compare your results to those of your peers. How do your results compare?
- Analyse and evaluate your test results. Prepare charts or graphs to show the main results and trends. What conclusions can you draw?
- Using one test result for each component of fitness, suggest appropriate recommendations you could make to your own fitness levels.
- Suggest three different training methods you could use to help achieve your fitness goals, and give reasons for your choice.

One-minute sit-up test (muscular endurance)

This test is used to assess the endurance and development of your abdominal muscles.

What you will need

- Access to an indoor sports hall
- Exercise mat
- Stopwatch

Method

1 Lie on a mat with your knees bent and feet flat on the floor, with your arms folded across your body.

2 Raise yourself up to a 90-degree position, then return to the floor.

3 Your feet may be held by a partner if you wish.

4 Record the total number of sit-ups for one minute.

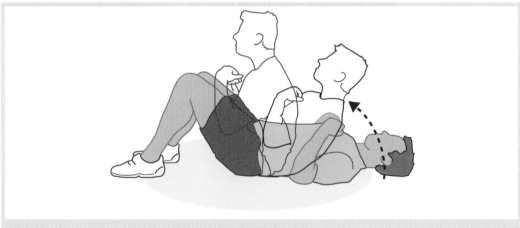

Figure 1.10 Participant performing the one-minute sit-up test

Interpreting results

Use Table 1.23 to interpret your results.

Table 1.23 One-minute sit-up test results

Rating	Males (no. of reps)	Females (no. of reps)
Excellent	49–59	42–54
Good	43–48	36–41
Above average	39–42	32–35
Average	35–38	28–31
Below average	31–34	24–27
Poor	25–30	18–23
Very poor	11–24	3–17

CONTINUED ▸▸

◤ Body Mass Index (BMI) (body composition)

This test is used to give a simple measure of body fat and is used to check whether a person is overweight.

The test can determine if a person is at increased risk of developing coronary heart disease (CHD) and other cardiovascular diseases.

BMI is widely used for the general population to determine the degree of overweight.

However, the test isn't always valid for elite sports performers and athletes, because it doesn't take into account frame size or muscle mass.

If a body builder had their BMI measured, they would be classed as obese; their large frame size and high muscle mass would give an invalid test result.

What you will need

- **Height stadiometer**
- Weighing scales

Method

1 Measure your body weight in kilograms (kg).

2 Measure your height in metres (m).

3 Carry out this calculation to determine your BMI (kg/m²):

$$BMI = \frac{\textbf{Body weight (kg)}}{\textbf{Height (m)} \times \textbf{Height (m)}}$$

4 Interpreting results:

Use Table 1.24 to interpret your results.

Table 1.24 BMI: interpreting results

Rating	BMI (kg/m²)
Desirable	20–25
Overweight	26–30
Obese and increased risk of CHD	31+

Bioelectrical Impedance Analysis (BIA) (body composition)

This test is used to predict % body fat.

A BIA machine is required to conduct the test (such as Bodystat 1500). The method is based on the fact that fat-free mass in the body (muscle, bone, connective tissues) conducts electricity, whereas fat mass does not. Therefore, the higher the resistance to a weak electrical current (bioelectrical impedance) the higher the % body fat of the individual.

Hydration levels can affect validity of test results. To ensure the test is valid, the subject should not:

- exercise for 12 hours prior to the test
- drink or eat within 4 hours of the test
- drink caffeine prior to the test.

What you will need

- A **bioelectrical impedance analysis (BIA)** machine

Method

1 The participant should urinate 30 minutes prior to conducting the test.
2 The participant should lie down and remove their right sock and shoe.
3 Place the BIA electrodes on the right wrist, right hand, right ankle and right foot.
4 Attach the cable leads (crocodile clips) to the exposed tabs on the electrodes.
5 Enter data into the BIA machine (e.g. participant's age, gender, height, weight, activity level).
6 The participant should lie still as the weak electrical current is passed through their body. The test only takes a few seconds.
7 The % body fat test result will be shown on the LCD display of the BIA machine.

Interpreting results

Use Table 1.25 to interpret the results.

Key term

Bioelectrical impedance analysis (BIA) – method used for measuring body composition.

Table 1.25 Interpreting % body fat test results

Rating	Males % body fat (16–29 years)	Females % body fat (16–29 years)
Very low fat	<7	<13
Slim	7–12	13–20
Ideal	13–17	21–25
Overweight	18–28	26–32
Obese	>28	>32

CONTINUED ▶▶

Key terms

Anterior auxiliary line – the crease at which the top of your arm, when hanging down, meets the chest.

Umbilicus – belly button.

Acromion process – the outer end of the scapula, forming the highest point of the shoulder.

Olecranon process – bony projection at the elbow.

Skinfold testing (body composition)

In this section you will be using the Jackson–Pollock nomogram method to predict % body fat. Following a standard method will help to ensure your results are valid.

Work in pairs or small groups for skinfold testing. Measurements should be taken on dry skin on the right side of the body. Exceptions to this would be if the participant has a tattoo or deformity on the site location, in which case the left side of the body would need to be used.

What you will need

- Skinfold calipers (such as Harpenden or SlimGuide)
- Tape measure
- A pen to mark the sites

Method

1 The participant should keep their muscles relaxed during the test.

2 Mark each skinfold site with a pen and use a tape measure to find the midpoints.

3 Grasp the skinfold firmly between your thumb and index finger, about 1cm away from the site marked, and gently pull away from the body.

4 Place the skinfold calipers perpendicular to the fold, on the site marked, with the dial facing upwards.

5 Maintaining your grasp, place the calipers midway between the base and tip of the skinfold and allow the calipers to be fully released so that full tension is placed on the skinfold.

6 Read the dial of the skinfold calipers to the nearest 0.5mm, 2 seconds after you have released the calipers. Make sure you continue to grasp the skinfold throughout testing.

7 Take a minimum of two measurements at each site. If repeated tests vary by more than 1mm, repeat the measurement. If consecutive measurements become smaller, this means that the fat is being compressed, and will result in inaccurate results. If this happens, go to another site and return to the first site later.

8 Make sure you record each measurement as it is taken.

9 The final value is the average of the two readings (mm).

Males: skinfold site selection

Male participants will need to gain skinfold results (mm) for the following three sites:

- **Chest** – a diagonal fold, half the distance between the **anterior auxiliary line** and the nipple.
- **Abdomen** – a vertical fold, 2cm to the right side of the **umbilicus**.
- **Thigh** – a vertical fold on the front of the thigh, halfway between the hip joint and the middle of the kneecap. The leg needs to be straight and relaxed.

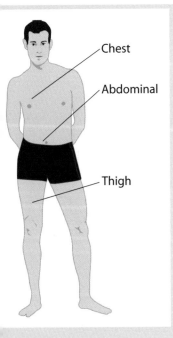

Figure 1.11 Site locations for males

Females: skinfold site selection

Female participants will need to gain skinfold results (mm) for the following three sites:

- **Triceps** – a vertical fold on the back midline of the upper arm, over the triceps muscle, halfway between the **acromion process** and **olecranon process**. The arm should be held freely by the side of the body.
- **Suprailiac** – a diagonal fold just above the hip bone and 2–3cm forward.
- **Thigh** – a vertical fold, on the front of the thigh, halfway between the hip joint and the middle of the kneecap. The leg needs to be straight and relaxed.

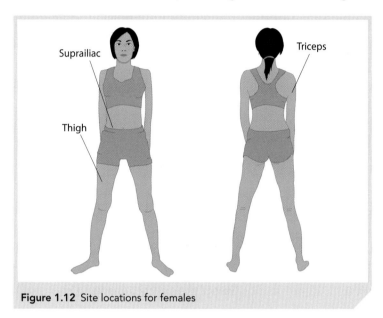

Figure 1.12 Site locations for females

Processing and interpreting results

1 Add up the sum of your three skinfolds (mm).
2 Obtain the % body fat result by plotting your age in years and the sum of the three skinfolds (mm) on the nomogram.
3 Use a ruler and sharpened pencil to join up the two points, which will cross over the % body fat (wavy) vertical lines.
4 Read your % body fat result to the nearest 0.5% according to your gender.
5 Use Table 1.25 to interpret the % body fat result obtained.

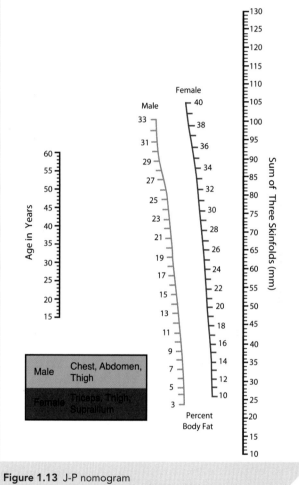

Figure 1.13 J-P nomogram

Assessment practice 1.6

1 Rob is 18 years old. He reached Level 12 Shuttle 12 in the multistage fitness test. Use Table 1.16 on page 29 to predict Rob's VO₂ max. Then use Tables 1.14 and 1.15 on page 28 to interpret Rob's aerobic endurance test result. (2)

2 Ana has just completed the Forestry step test. Her 15 second pulse count is 33. Ana is 15 years old and weighs 59kg. Use Tables 1.17b–d on pages 32–33 to work out and interpret Ana's VO₂ max (ml/kg/min). (2)

3 Pablo weighs 84kg and is 1.84m tall. Calculate and interpret Pablo's BMI (kg/m²) using Table 1.24 on page 38. (2)

Assessment Zone

This section has been written to help you to do your best when you take the onscreen test. Read through it carefully and ask your teacher if there is anything you are still not sure about.

How you will be assessed

You will take an onscreen assessment, using a computer. This will be set over 15-20 screens and have a maximum of 50 marks. The number of marks for each question will be shown in brackets e.g. [1]. The test will last for one hour.

There will be different types of question in the test:

Disclaimer: These practice questions and sample answers are not actual exam questions. They are provided as a practice aid only and should not be assumed to reflect either the format or coverage of the real external test.

A Questions where the answers are available and you have to choose the correct answer(s). *Tip: always read carefully to see how many answers are needed and how you can show the right answer.*

Examples:

> Which **two** of the following are components of skill-related fitness? Select the two correct answers. [2]
>
> | **A** | Agility |
> | **B** | Flexibility |
> | **C** | Body composition |
> | **D** | Aerobic endurance |
> | **E** | Balance |
>
> Answers: A and E

> Sharon is 27 years old and has just started training at her local gym. Calculate Sharon's maximum heart rate (HRmax). Select the correct answer. [1]
>
> | **A** | 193 bpm |
> | **B** | 173 bpm |
> | **C** | 183 bpm |
> | **D** | 203 bpm |
>
> Answer: A

B Questions where you are asked to provide a short answer worth 1–2 marks. *Tip: Look carefully at how the question is set out to see how many points need to be included in your answer.*

Examples:

> Louise reports an RPE of 17. What will her approximate heart rate be? [1]
>
> Answer: 170 bpm

> Name **two** types of static stretching. [2]
>
> Answers: Active stretching and passive stretching

C Questions where you are asked to provide a longer answer – these can be worth up to 8 marks. *Tip: Plan your answer, making sure that you include the correct level of detail indicated by the amount of marks allocated. Check through your answer – you may need to use the scroll bar to move back to the top.*

Example:

> Agility is an important component of fitness for a footballer. Explain how two other components of fitness can contribute to success in football. [4]
>
> **Answer:** Aerobic endurance is needed so the player can 'keep-up' with the pace of the game, so they can run efficiently for the full duration of a match, creating opportunities on the pitch for his/her team mates.
>
> Strength is needed so the footballer can perform effective tackles/blocks, allowing them to maintain position without being nudged off the ball.

Many questions will have images. Sometimes you will be asked to click to play a video or animation. You can do this as many times as you want within the time allowed for the test.

Sometimes you may be asked to do a calculation – you can use the calculator provided in the onscreen test system if you need to.

Hints and tips

- **Use the pre-test time** – make sure you have read the instructions, tested the function buttons, adjusted your seat and that you can see the screen clearly.
- **Watch the time** – the screen shows you how much time you have left. You should aim to take about 1 minute per mark. Some early questions will take less time than this and some later questions will take you longer.
- **Plan your longer answers** - read the question carefully and think about the key points you will make. You can use paper or the onscreen note function to jot down ideas.
- **Check answers at the end** – you should keep moving through the questions and not let yourself get stuck on one. If you are really unsure of answer or cannot give an answer, then you can use the onscreen system to flag that you need to come back to that question at the end.
- **Read back your longer answers** – make sure you view the whole answer if you are checking back. There is no spell check facility.
- **Do you find it harder to read onscreen?** – talk to your teacher/tutor in advance of your test about how the system can be adjusted to meet your needs. During the test, tools within the test player will allow you to apply colour filters, change the font size and colour, as well as allowing you to zoom in on the images and text.

How to improve your answer

Read the two student answers below, together with the feedback. Try to use what you learn here when you answer questions in your test.

Question

Patrick and David are 20 years old. They are both keen amateur basketball players and would like to begin training with a new coach.

a) The new coach has identified two fitness tests which could be used to determine Patrick's and David's baseline levels of fitness. Explain why the coach would have chosen each of these tests:
  - Vertical jump test [2]
  - Illinois agility test [2]

b) Describe how one method of training could be used to develop and improve their performance in basketball. [2]

Student 1's answer

a) The vertical jump test can be used to determine a player's anaerobic power. The Illinois agility run test could be used because this test can be used to determine a player's speed and agility.

b) They could use plyometric training.

Feedback:

a) *For each test, an attempt has been made at justifying its selection in relation to fitness components. However, the learner has not strengthened their justifications by linking these fitness tests and components of fitness to their importance for a basketball player, so only 1 mark is awarded for each explanation rather than 2 marks. For part a) the student would achieve 2 marks.*

b) *The student has correctly identified that plyometric training could be used by the basketball players, but has not provided any further details on how it could actually improve their performance. For part b) the student would achieve 1 mark.*

Student 2's answer

a) The vertical jump test could be used because it can determine a player's anaerobic power, which is important for their jumping ability when dunking or intercepting a pass. The Illinois agility run test could be used, because this test can determine a player's speed and agility, which are important so they can run a fast-break, stop, start or change directions quickly to avoid an opponent, moving quickly and efficiently around the basketball court.

b) Plyometric training would be a great way for Patrick and David to develop their basketball skills and overall performance on the court. They could use bounding, hopping and jumping drills to develop explosive power and strength, helping improve their jumping ability to score baskets and their sprinting ability to drive to the basket before opponents catch up.

Feedback:

a) *The learner has justified the choice of the two fitness tests by linking these tests to the components of fitness (1 mark) and also their importance for success in basketball (1 mark). For part a) the student will achieve 2 marks for each test, totalling 4 marks.*

b) *The student has correctly stated that plyometric training could be used by the basketball players (1 mark). They have described what this training method could involve (1 mark), with further details on how this training method could actually improve performance (1 mark). For part b) the student will achieve 3 marks.*

Assess yourself

Question 1

Body fat can be predicted using the Jackson-Pollock (J-P) Nomogram method. This method uses three skinfold sites for females.

Select the **three** correct skinfold sites for **females** from the list below [3].

Suprailiac
Chest
Thigh
Triceps
Subcapular

Question 2

Fitness testing can play an important part in an athlete's training cycle.

a) Name the piece of fitness testing equipment shown in the photograph [1].

b) State the component of fitness this piece of equipment is used to test [1].

c) State the units of measurement [1].

Question 3

Describe how a greater range of movement is achieved using the PNF technique. [2]

For further practice, see the Assessment Practice questions on pages 5, 7, 9, 19, 25 and 41.

Introduction

Participation in sport is growing, as people become more aware of the benefits of physical activity. This unit focuses on developing and improving your own practical sports performance. You will be given the opportunity to participate in selected sports and carry out skills, techniques and tactics in different situations within those sports.

Through your participation you will develop knowledge of the rules, regulations and scoring systems associated with these sports and how to apply them, and you will be introduced to the roles and responsibilities of sporting officials.

High-achieving sports performers reflect on their own performance to identify what they are good at (their strengths) and also assess the areas of their performance they need to develop (areas for improvement). As you progress through this unit you will develop an understanding of the processes for reviewing your own performance and finding ways to improve your skills.

Assessment: You will be assessed by a series of assignments set by your teacher/tutor.

Learning aims

In this unit you will:

A understand the rules, regulations and scoring systems for selected sports

B practically demonstrate skills, techniques and tactics in selected sports

C be able to review sports performance.

"I had rarely played hockey before and never thought I would be good enough to play for a team. It was only when I was given the opportunity to play practice matches and develop a further understanding of the sport as part of my BTEC Sport course at school that I was asked to join a local club.

Ben, *16-year-old club hockey player*

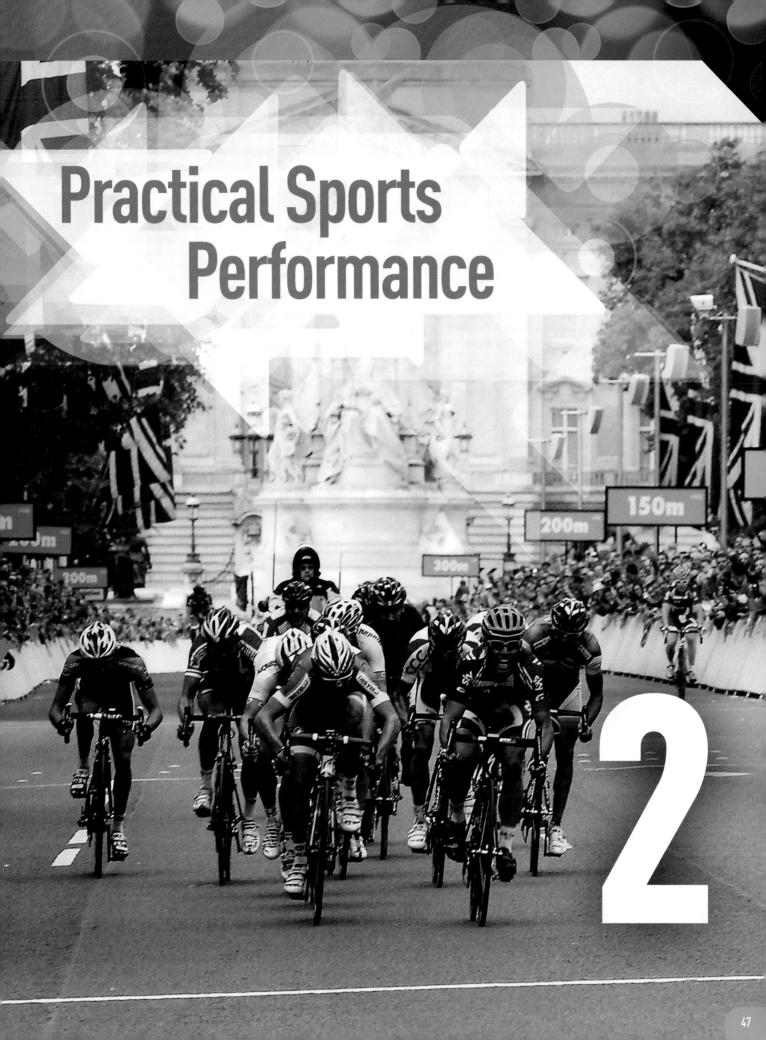

Practical Sports Performance

2

BTEC
Assessment zone

This table shows you what you must do in order to achieve a **Pass**, **Merit** or **Distinction** grade, and where you can find activities to help you.

Assessment criteria			
Level 1	**Level 2 Pass**	**Level 2 Merit**	**Level 2 Distinction**
Learning aim A: understand the rules, regulations and scoring systems for selected sports			
1A.1 English Describe the rules, regulations and scoring systems of a selected sport	**2A.P1** English Describe the rules, regulations and scoring systems of two selected sports **See Assessment activity 2.1, page 57**	**2A.M1** English For each of two selected sports, explain the roles and responsibilities of officials and the application of rules, regulations and scoring systems **See Assessment activity 2.1, page 57**	**2A.D1** English Compare and contrast the roles and responsibilities of officials from two selected sports, suggesting valid recommendations for improvement to the application of rules, regulations and scoring systems for each sport **See Assessment activity 2.1, page 57**
1A.2 Apply the rules of a selected sport in two given specific situations	**2A.P2** Apply the rules of a selected sport in four specific situations **See Assessment activity 2.1, page 57**		
1A.3 Describe the roles of officials from a selected sport	**2A.P3** Describe the roles and responsibilities of officials from two selected sports **See Assessment activity 2.1, page 57**		
Learning aim B: practically demonstrate skills, techniques and tactics in selected sports			
1B.4 Describe the technical demands of two selected sports	**2B.P4** Describe the technical and tactical demands of two selected sports **See Assessment activity 2.2, page 69**		
1B.5 Use relevant skills and techniques effectively, in two selected sports, in isolated practices	**2B.P5** Use relevant skills, techniques and tactics effectively, in two selected sports, in conditioned practices **See Assessment activity 2.2, page 69**	**2B.M2** Use relevant skills, techniques and tactics effectively, in two selected sports, in competitive situations **See Assessment activity 2.2, page 69**	

Assessment criteria			
Level 1	**Level 2 Pass**	**Level 2 Merit**	**Level 2 Distinction**
Learning aim C: be able to review sports performance			
1C.6 English Produce, with guidance, an observation checklist that can be used effectively to review own performance in two selected sports	**2C.P6** English Independently produce an observation checklist that can be used effectively to review own performance in two selected sports **See Assessment activity 2.3, page 73**		
1C.7 Review own performance, in two selected sports, identifying strengths and areas for improvement	**2C.P7** Review own performance, in two selected sports, describing strengths and areas for improvement **See Assessment activity 2.3, page 73**	**2C.M3** Explain strengths and areas for improvement in two selected sports, recommending activities to improve own performance **See Assessment activity 2.3, page 73**	**2C.D2** Analyse strengths and areas for improvement in two selected sports, justifying recommended activities to improve own performance **See Assessment activity 2.3, page 73**

English Opportunity to practise English skills

How you will be assessed

Your knowledge and understanding of this unit will be checked through a series of assignments set by your teacher/tutor. You will be expected to show that you understand the rules, regulations and scoring systems for selected sports, and how to apply these in given situations. You will also be required to demonstrate knowledge of the roles and responsibilities of officials. You will then be observed and assessed for your ability to use skills, techniques and tactics while playing sports, and will need to show that you know how to review your own performance to identify your strengths and weaknesses.

Your assessment could be in the form of:

- practical demonstrations
- verbal/written work to show understanding of rules, regulations and roles of officials
- observation checklists.

Rules (or laws) in sport

Getting started

Make a list of five rules which you have to abide by in your school/college. Discuss how these rules are implemented and what happens if you break each rule. Who implements these rules within the school/college?

Key terms

Sport – an activity such as athletics, hockey, netball or swimming that involves physical exertion, skill, competition and rules.

National Governing Body (NGB) – an organisation responsible for the promotion and development of a particular sport at a national level.

International Governing Body (IGB) – an organisation responsible for the promotion and development of a particular sport at an international level. For example, FIFA.

Introduction

All **sports** have set rules or laws. It is these rules that determine the format of the game and provide structure and discipline.

Rules are determined by the International Governing Body for each sport. It is the role of **National Governing Bodies (NGBs)** in the UK to work closely with these **International Governing Bodies (IGBs)** to ensure that rules are observed by officials, clubs and performers during organised competitions.

In the past ten years a number of sports have announced some changes to the rules to make events more entertaining for the spectators. For example, in 2011 the International Association of Athletics Federations (IAAF) adapted the rules for false starts, changing the original rule from giving all athletes a warning if there was a false start in a race to having no warning procedure; in the event of a false start, the athlete who commits it is instantly disqualified. This rule change came under a high level of scrutiny in the World Athletics Championships in Daegu in 2011 when in the 100 metres final Usain Bolt was disqualified for committing a false start in the race. In most sports rules are updated regularly, and it is the responsibility of everybody involved in a sport to have a thorough knowledge of these changes.

Due to the high number of participants in certain sports, some NGBs require Regional Governing Bodies to support the coordination and organisation of sport at regional level. For example, in football each county in England has its own Football Association. In East Yorkshire the East Riding County FA (ERCFA) organise all leagues and competitions that are played within that region. It is the role of ERCFA to administer all football played within the county in line with the Football Association's guidance and support.

Table 2.1 Different sports have different National Governing Bodies (NGBs)

Sport	NGB	Website
Football	The Football Association	www.thefa.com
Rugby union	The Rugby Football Union	www.rfu.com
Rugby league	The Rugby Football League	www.therfl.co.uk
Athletics	UK Athletics	www.uka.org.uk
Orienteering	British Orienteering	www.britishorienteering.org.uk
Skiing	Snow Sport England	www.snowsportengland.org.uk

Every sport must have an NGB. If your preferred sport is not listed in the table above, research it and add details of its NGB to a table like Table 2.1.

FIFA:
Fédération Internationale de Football Association

AFC:
Asian Football Confederation
(Asia)

CAF:
Confédération Africaine de Football
(Africa)

CONCACAF:
Confederation of North, Central America and Caribbean Association Football

CONMEBOL:
Confederación Sudamericana de Fútbol
(South America)

OFC:
Oceania Football Confederation

UEFA:
Union of Europe Football Associations

Other European national associations

FA:
The Football Association
(England)

Figure 2.1 Chart showing the organisation of football across the world

Activity 2.1 Finding out about Governing Bodies

1 Research the Regional Football Association closest to your school. Provide an address and telephone number for the Regional Office.
2 Identify the National Governing Bodies for three other sports and identify whether or not there are any regional governing bodies within your local area.

Unwritten rules

As well as sports having written rules there are also some underpinning values that are associated with all sports. These values, known as the unwritten rules, contribute towards fair play. The concept of fair play includes:

- respect towards other sports performers
- respect towards coaches and spectators
- respect towards officials
- playing within the rules of the sport
- equality for all sports performers.

Applying fair play in sport, and promoting the concept of fair play at all levels, can help to reduce some of the negative elements of sport such as violence, verbal abuse, physical abuse and gamesmanship, whereby players cheat to gain an advantage; for example, by doping.

In football, the handshake is a common way of showing respect for another player.

Just checking

1 Summarise five major rules that you are required to know and understand in order to play your chosen sport.
2 What is the role of a National Governing Body?
3 What is the NGB in the United Kingdom for athletics?

Regulations in sport

Link

See *Topic A.1* for more information on governing bodies.

Key term

Regulations – rules in sport that are controlled by an authority (a National Governing Body).

Tennis is played at the highest level on a variety of surfaces (grass, clay and hard courts).

Introduction

Regulations are the rules or principles that are applied consistently in a sport. These differ across all sports, which is why each sport requires a regulator, or Governing Body.

Players and participants

Different sports have different numbers of players participating in competitive situations. Sports such as golf, tennis, gymnastics and athletics are usually considered individual sports (with some exceptions – e.g. doubles in tennis, relays in athletics). Other sports such as rugby union, hockey, basketball and American football, are team sports. These sports have restrictions on the numbers of players allowed in a competitive situation at any one time.

Playing surfaces

Some NGBs and IGBs dictate the surface types on which a sport can be played. For example, in the sport of rugby league the International Governing Body, until very recently, ruled that competitive games must be played on grass pitches. It was only in the 2012 season that Widnes Vikings were allowed to introduce the first artificial pitch into the European Super League. However, some sports can be played both inside and outside, and the requirements for the types of surfaces may differ. For example, after many years of research and more than two decades of preventing the use of artificial surfaces in football, in 2005 the Union of European Football Associations (UEFA) approved the use of a new artificial surface, known as the third generation pitch (3G), to be used within all their competitions.

Equipment

In one form or another all sports require equipment. It may be the specific protective equipment which the performers are required to wear to reduce or prevent injury. For example, in the sport of track cycling all participants must wear helmets when competing. Or it may be the equipment which is required to play the sport, such as the goalposts in a football game or a rugby game, the racket in tennis, the high jump bar, starter blocks and track in athletics, or the bicycle in mountain biking.

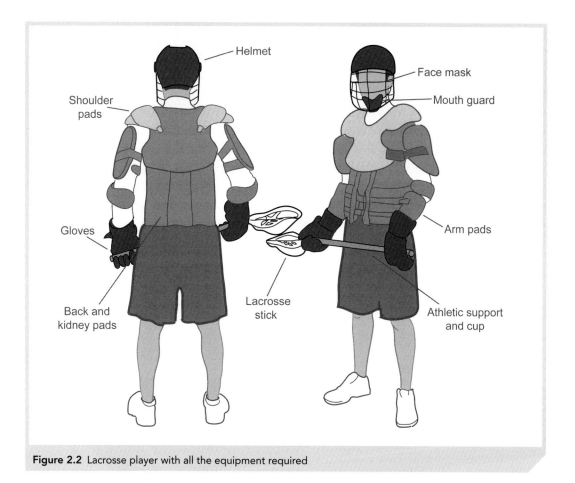

Figure 2.2 Lacrosse player with all the equipment required

Labels: Helmet, Shoulder pads, Gloves, Back and kidney pads, Lacrosse stick, Face mask, Mouth guard, Arm pads, Athletic support and cup

---

Activity 2.2 What equipment is needed?

1 Provide the list of equipment which may be required for a cricket player, in order to ensure that the player is both safe and playing the game in line with the rules of the sport.

2 For your own sport provide a list of the equipment which is required in line with the rules of the sport and the equipment that players wear in order to protect themselves from injury.

Health and safety

Many rules and regulations within sports have evolved to prevent the risk of injuries to sports performers. This continues to be the case in all sports. For example, in June 2008 the FA brought out further regulations with regards to goalpost safety, which applied to all football clubs. See the FA website for more details, please go to Pearson Hotlinks (www.pearsonhotlinks.co.uk) and search for this BTEC Sport title.

CONTINUED ▶▶

◤ Facilities

One of the key regulations in sport involves the court, pool, course, track, ring or pitch layout. It is up to the governing bodies to agree on the dimensions of the playing area in order for a competition to take place. Some sports are more flexible when it comes to the size of the playing area and its surface, whereas other sports are very strict regarding these dimensions. For example, FINA (International Swimming Federation) state that all international competitions use a 50 metre Olympic-style pool, whereas FIFA (International Football Federation) state that football can be played on slightly different-sized pitches as long as they are between 90 metres and 120 metres long and 45 metres and 90 metres wide, although the goals must be of a standard size.

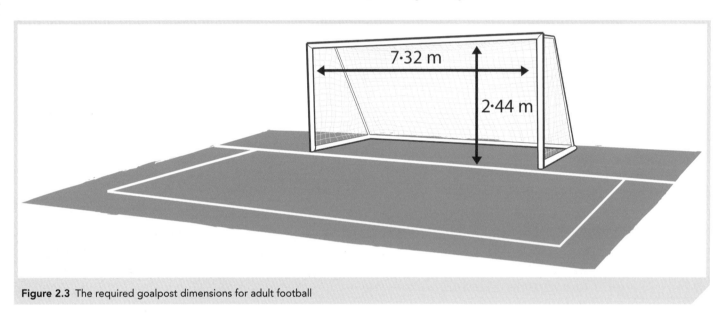

Figure 2.3 The required goalpost dimensions for adult football

◤ Time

Most team sports have a restriction on the duration of matches or competitions. This time is often divided into equal periods. For example, England Basketball have determined that all games competed within the England Basketball league are played in four quarters of 10 minutes each. This gives teams sufficient time to attempt to outscore the opposing team. In sports such as basketball, there is also an option to stop the clock and discuss tactics and make alterations (a 'time out'). In other sports, e.g. football, the only time tactical instructions can be made to the whole team is during the allocated breaks. In football, this break is called 'half-time'.

In some sports competitions, when the scores are even at the end of 'normal' time, 'extra' time is played to determine a winner. If there is no clear winner after extra time, some sports have a final method of concluding the match. An example of this is the use of sudden-death extra time in rugby league knock-out cup competitions such as the Challenge Cup. Play is ended when either team scores a point (drop goal, penalty conversion or try) to finally win the game outright.

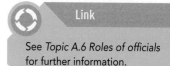

For other sports, a winner can be confirmed before the allocated time has run out. A test match in cricket is allocated five full days; however, each side is only allocated two innings each. So if one team scores 500 runs in one innings after one day and on the second day the other team is bowled out for 50 and instructed to follow on and is bowled out again for 150 on the same day, the match is over – the team first in to bat has won the fixture.

Link

See *Topic A.6 Roles of officials* for further information.

Officials

Officials have clear roles and responsibilities regarding the application of the rules and regulations for a sport as stated by the Governing Body.

Scoring systems

Every sport has a different method of scoring. In most games the performer or team who scores the most points within a designated time period, or who reaches a certain number of points, is the winner. The main exception to this is golf, where the winner is the player who hits the lowest number of shots.

However, some sports require a different method of scoring, such as athletics where a performer is measured on times, distances and heights, depending on the discipline. Gymnastics events are scored using a subjective scoring method, where performances are assessed against the perfect model through the eyes of judges.

Every sport has clear rules that determine victory. It is important that as a performer in a sport you are aware of the requirements of winning.

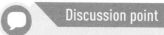

Discussion point

In your sport, what happens if the scores are tied at the end of normal time – how is the contest decided? Is this method of extra time applied in all competitive matches or just in specific competitions?

Figure 2.4 Baseball scoreboard

Activity 2.3	Scoring systems

Select two sports.

1 For each sport highlight the scoring systems that are applied.
2 Identify any different methods of scoring that may be applied to alternative competitions (e.g. doubles in tennis).
3 Can you think of any methods of developing the scoring systems within each sport to make the sport more entertaining?

Just checking

1 What size of pool must be used for international swimming competitions?
2 Make a list of the different playing surfaces that tennis can be played upon competitively.
3 List three officials required in your own selected sport.

Application of the rules/laws of sports

Look at the image of a rugby referee applying the rules of rugby. It is important to follow the rules, laws and regulations of sport and apply the appropriate sanctions. In this instance the player is receiving a yellow card for spear-tackling an opponent. Discuss rules in your sport that can result in dismissal or a warning from the referee.

Introduction

As well as understanding the rules, laws and regulations of your selected sport, you need to develop knowledge of how to apply these within specific situations. This will require you to take the role of the official within a competitive situation and demonstrate how to apply the rules, laws and regulations.

When applying rules and regulations in a specific situation you will need to ensure that you use the correct method of communication to stop the game and take the correct action against the performer or team. It is important that you justify the reasons behind your decision within each situation.

For example, when a player breaks a rule in basketball the referee communicates that a rule has been broken by using a whistle to stop play. The official then uses a hand signal to communicate to all players, spectators and coaches which rule has been broken. Finally, the official verbally communicates the sanction to the player involved.

Officials have other methods of communicating with players, spectators and coaches in other sports. An assistant referee in football will wave a flag in a certain way to demonstrate that a rule has been broken or to stop play.

A rugby referee awarding a yellow card to a player during a rugby match

A badminton line judge will shout to communicate with players and spectators. They will also produce a hand signal to communicate their decision with the players, spectators and coaches who are observing. In sports where there is the use of an off-field umpire the decision may be communicated using technology. For example, in rugby league when the video referee makes a decision the result of the decision is displayed on a television screen for the on-field officials, players, coaches and spectators to see all at the same time.

In football an assistant referee will use their flag to demonstrate that a rule has been broken.

Table 2.2 gives examples of situations in which officials would need to take action.

Table 2.2 Situations in which rules would need to be applied in certain sports

Sport	Situation
Football	A goal is scored when a player is in an offside position
Cricket	The ball hitting the batsman's legs directly in front of the wickets before hitting the bat
Basketball	Charging in lead-up to scoring
Rugby league/ union	Forward pass resulting in a try
Hockey	The ball running behind the end line after touching a defender
Tennis	The ball landing in the court boundaries after hitting the net post during a rally

Assessment activity 2.1   *English*   2A.P1 | 2A.P2 | 2A.P3 | 2A.M1 | 2A.D1

The PE coordinator from a local primary school has asked you to help the Year 6 students with their understanding of the rules and scoring systems for two sports.

1 Develop a short video that gives information about the following for two sports of your choice:

  • the rules, regulations and scoring systems
  • the roles and responsibilities of the officials.

2 Are there similarities and differences between the roles and responsibilities of the officials? Can you recommend ways to improve the application of the rules, regulations and scoring systems?

3 For the next part of the video, select one of these sports and take the role of a referee. You should demonstrate how the rules are applied correctly in four situations.

Tips
  • Provide examples to show how each official applies the rules effectively within competitive situations.
  • Give your ideas for how the rules of each sport could be developed to make the sport more entertaining – consider methods of scoring and other rules which could be adapted to make the game more exciting.
  • You will need to demonstrate the methods of communication used to apply these rules in each of the situations.

Roles of officials

Introduction

Different sports require different types of **official**, each with their own **roles** and responsibilities. Some sports require more officials than there are players, such as tennis, in which there are up to eleven people officiating during a competitive match. In other sports there may be very few officials.

Umpires

An example of a sport that uses umpires is cricket. Traditionally there will be two umpires per match and they are in charge of all decisions made on the pitch. For example, the umpire makes the decisions regarding whether or not a batsman is out, or whether a shot has been hit for four or six runs. The umpires ensure that the match is played in accordance with the laws of the game.

Key terms

Official – a representative of a National Governing Body who applies the rules of a specific sport in competitive situations.

Role – the actions and activities assigned to or required or expected of a person.

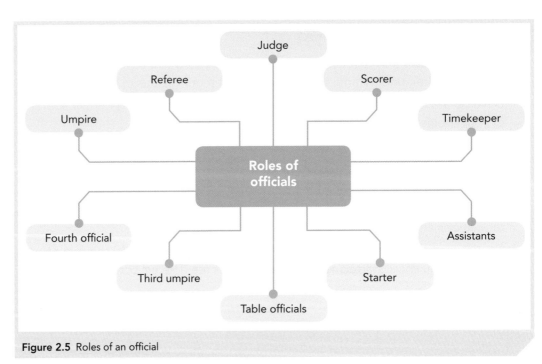

Figure 2.5 Roles of an official

Figure 2.6 Examples of hand signals that a cricket umpire uses.

Referees

The role of the referee is to ensure that all of the rules (or laws) of the game are followed by performers. The referee can apply the rules on the field of play, although a referee can also manage the game from off-field.

An example of a referee who is on the field of play and constantly making decisions that affect the end result is a lacrosse referee. An example of a referee who is off the field of play is a volleyball referee.

Judges

Sports such as gymnastics and boxing use judges to **officiate**. In gymnastics, the judge observes the performance of the athlete and assesses the demonstration of the skill or technique against a set of **criteria**. These are based on a perfect model of the skill or technique. A boxing judge will observe the performance of a boxer competing in a ring and will award points for every clean punch connected, or at the end of each round award victory to one of the boxers. Rounds can also be drawn if the judge deems that there is no clear winner. In each case, the judge makes a decision based on observations.

Key terms

Officiate – to administer the rules and control the game, race or match.

Criteria – a standard by which a sports performer is judged.

Did you know?

In rugby union there are four officials (including the video referee) and 30 players on the pitch at any one time. Each official has a specific role to carry out during a competitive situation.

Which rules of tennis does a line judge apply during a competitive game of tennis?

Timekeepers

Some sports have a restriction on the amount of time allocated to a match or competitive situation. In basketball there are official timekeepers to record the duration of the game and to start and stop the clock at specific stages of the game. For some sports it is a requirement that every time the ball is out of play or play stops, time is stopped and not started again until play resumes. The timekeeper has the sole responsibility to stop and start the clock.

Starters

In sports such as swimming and athletics the starter plays a vital role. It is the starter who informs the participants in a race when to start. The starter is also in charge of monitoring false starts and sanctioning performers appropriately when the starting rules are broken. In many sports the starter also has the responsibility to verbally communicate with the performers and prepare them for the start of the race.

Activity 2.4   List of officials

For your sport, provide a list of the officials who are involved in applying the rules of the sport and also include a summary of the rules that each official applies during a competitive situation. You could present your findings in a table.

Responsibilities of officials

Getting started

Select an official from your own sport. Complete a 10 point guide of what makes them an effective official in your selected sport – look at how many responsibilities you have covered within your 10 point guide.

Introduction

Officials in each sport have a defined set of responsibilities.

Appearance

For most sports it is a requirement that officials wear a specific uniform. This uniform differentiates them from the performers and reinforces their importance. The uniform worn by the officials must not clash with the colours of the sports performers.

Equipment

If specific equipment is required to support the application of the rules and regulations of the sport, it is each official's responsibility to bring the appropriate kit to every competition or game. For example, a netball umpire will need to arrive at a game equipped with a whistle, a scorecard, a stopwatch, a coin and a pen.

Equipment required by a football referee. Can you think of any other equipment that a football referee may require?

Did you know?

In most sports, the more qualifications you obtain as a referee/umpire the higher the level you can officiate in the selected sport.

Qualifications

For some sports, the official must hold a recognised officiating qualification. All National Governing Bodies provide training and qualifications to educate and develop existing officials. Properly trained officials help to ensure that the game is played within the laws stated and takes place in a safe and appropriate environment.

Activity 2.5   Find out about officiating courses

For one team sport and one individual sport of your choice, visit the NGB website and carry out some research into officiating courses for each (this will often be found under 'Education'). Make a list of the different courses and underline the one that you feel would be most appropriate for you.

Fitness

For some sports it is a requirement for officials to be on the field of play and keep up with the play to ensure that they are close at hand to make decisions and **sanction** performers as necessary. This requires a high level of fitness, as play can be very fast, and the official may even do more running than some of the players on the pitch.

Interpretation and application of the rules

One of the major responsibilities of an official in any sport is the ability to apply the rules and regulations. It is a requirement of all officials to observe the state of play carefully. If they spot that the rules of the sport have been broken, officials must take appropriate action and apply sanctions as stated within the laws of the sport.

It is important that the official is in the best position possible to make the correct decision. Officials have to be confident in the decisions that they make, as once a decision is made they should stand by it.

Control of players

An official will demonstrate control of the sports performers and ensure that they are safe during the competitive situation by applying regulations correctly and confidently. In some sports, if the laws are broken because of serious foul play the officials have the power to discipline the players by sending them off the field of play. Control can also be applied through effective communication.

Effective communication

In some sports there are numerous officials involved in competitive situations. It is important for them to communicate clearly, and listen carefully to each other. This is also necessary when officials are enforcing the rules or laws of a sport – the official should clearly inform the players about each decision made. An official who communicates effectively and confidently will gain respect from performers. In some sports a referee is also provided with a whistle as a tool for controlling the performers and applying the rules. In some instances specific sanctions may require specific whistle usage.

Key term

Sanction – a penalty which is awarded against a sports performer for breaking a rule.

Activity 2.6	The importance of the whistle

Referee a game of five-a-side football, basketball or hockey. For the first 5 minutes use a whistle and then for the next 5 minutes do not use a whistle. After the activity discuss the following points with the rest of your group.

1 Did you use the whistle effectively?

2 What was the response of the participants when you blew the whistle?

3 How did you communicate with the performers when the whistle was removed?

4 What was the most effective form of communication while officiating?

5 How could you develop your ability to officiate effectively?

CONTINUED ▶▶

Accountability to spectators

Spectators who observe sports often come to watch a specific individual or specific team. Therefore, it is important that the official demonstrates an unbiased opinion at all times.

An official should apply the rules and laws of sport equally to all competitors, using clear methods of communication to display which laws and rules have been broken.

Hawk-eye is now used in tennis if a player wants to challenge the umpire's decision.

Health and safety

A major responsibility of officials in sport is to ensure that every event is carried out safely, in order to protect players, spectators, coaches and officials.

Officials should carry out safety checks before, during and after a sports event.

These should include checks of:

- **Equipment** – to ensure that equipment is suitable, in good condition, and has no chance of causing injury to the sports performers.
- **Facilities** – the area in which the competition is going to take place must be safe for spectators. Playing surfaces must not pose a risk of injury to sports performers.
- **Players** – if an official feels at any time during a competitive situation that sports performers are under threat of injury or illness they have the responsibility to stop play and resolve the health and safety hazards.

Fair play

Officials should promote fair play at all times through respecting the sports performers that they are officiating, respecting the coaches and spectators observing the sport, and applying the rules fairly and consistently to both teams.

Use of technology

As technology has developed, more sports have moved towards using it to apply laws consistently.

For some sports the introduction of technology is still under debate. However, other sports have embraced the use of technology to support the officials who are on the field of play and may require a second opinion.

Cricket has introduced the **third umpire**, and rugby league and rugby union have introduced a **video referee**.

Key terms

Third umpire – an off-field umpire who makes the final decision in questions referred to him by the two on-field umpires. Television replays are available to the third umpire to assist him in making a decision.

Video referee – some sports allow referees to consult replay footage before making or revising a decision about unclear or dubious play. In rugby league and rugby union this person is called the video referee.

Discussion point

In your group discuss the advantages and disadvantages of goal-line technology.

WorkSpace

Denise Robinson

Basketball Level 1 referee (apprentice)

I have been a basketball official for my local basketball team for over two years now. As a basketball official I have the responsibility of keeping the score, updating the scoreboard and recording individual and team fouls. I have played basketball for a number of years and as I developed my own knowledge of the rules I became more confident.

When I was asked by my club if I was interested in helping out as a basketball official I was nervous initially, but over time my confidence has developed. The club also decided that I was good enough to officiate in some of the national league matches, but prior to doing this I had to attain the appropriate basketball official's qualification. It took me over a year to achieve both my Level 1 and Level 2 basketball official awards.

As a basketball official I have learned a lot more about the application of the rules of basketball through watching the floor officials apply the rules. It was observing the referees in charge of the game that actually made me want to become a referee. I have recently completed my Level 1 (apprentice) referee qualification with the NGB. Since gaining this award I have been able to officiate at school matches within my club.

I have found refereeing basketball very enjoyable and I hope to continue with this for the rest of my life. I see this as an opportunity to put something back into a sport which I truly love.

Think about it

1   When officiating, why is confidence so important?

2   In your sport can you identify the officials required in a competitive situation? Can you identify the rules and regulations that each of these officials have to apply during a competitive situation?

3   What courses would you need to undertake to become an official in your sport?

Technical demands of sport

Getting started

Select one skill from your sport and show your partner/rest of the group how to apply the skill effectively and successfully.

Key term

Skill – something that we learn how to do.

Introduction

Every sport requires specific **skills**; mastering the application of these skills supports the development of a sports performer. The skills you require will depend on the sport you play and in some sports these skills will be different. A skill is learned, and is not something we can do without coaching, training or observation of others. When we are first introduced to a skill it is often very difficult to master and takes a lot of physical and mental effort.

Figure 2.7 shows examples of some skills and techniques used in sports. For your own sport think about which of these are appropriate, and add any others as you see fit.

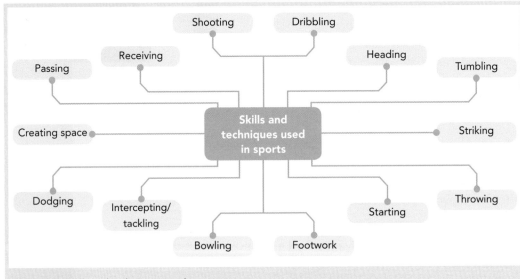

Figure 2.7 Skills and techniques used in sports

In sport we often use the word 'skilful' to identify a quality that a performer displays. This can sometimes be confused with performance. A hockey player who can demonstrate a variety of tricks while dribbling can be seen as skilful, but these skills are not a measurement of the ability to play hockey in a competitive scenario. A skilful player is someone who makes skills look easy, using very little effort, and who always applies skills successfully.

Skills in sport can be categorised as follows:

- **Continuous skills** are those that have no obvious beginning or end; they could be continued for as long as the performer wishes. For example, running.
- A **discrete skill** has a clear beginning and end. The skill can be repeated, but the performer will start the full action again in a controlled and timely manner. For example, a golf putt.
- A **serial skill** is a series of discrete skills that together produce an organised movement. The order of the movement is often very important but the requirements of each part of the skill will require specific development. For example, a gymnastic tumble.

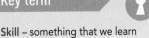

Sailors must become skilful at handling the ropes.

Activity 2.7 — Listing skill requirements

Cricket is a game where different skills are required within different components of the game.

1 List the skills and techniques required for the following roles:

- batsman
- bowler
- fielder.

2 For your own sport (or another sport) complete the same activity, listing all the different positions (if appropriate) and the skills, techniques and abilities required for each.

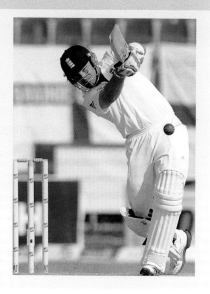

 # Movement

The ability to move efficiently and effectively around the designated area of play is very important in some sports (for example, tennis and volleyball). The more efficiently a sports performer can move around the court or pitch, the more time they have to apply the appropriate skills within a competitive situation.

 # Use of equipment

In sports there is an additional requirement for performers to master the use of equipment to compete in the sport effectively. For example, when mountain biking the rider of the bike has to develop the skill to use the bike effectively to maximise their performance during a race. The level of technique can often determine the performer's ability level.

Communication and interaction

The ability to communicate with other people when competing in sport as part of a team is a very important skill. Sports performers use various methods of **interaction** in a competitive situation to get the best result for the team.

In rugby union the forwards will rehearse the line-outs during their training sessions. The team might apply code words or non-verbal signs to indicate to their players where the ball will be directed to in the line-out. The ability to master this effectively is a skill.

 # Other demands

In some sports there are other demands to consider. These may not be a physical requirement but rather a mental challenge. For example, in orienteering, prior to completing the planned course, the competitors need to plan their route. Such meticulous forward planning can provide the edge over other competitors completing the same course.

 Discussion point

In your group, make a list of sports that require performers to use equipment. Also in your group look at a sport that the majority of the group has played and discuss the issues around learning how to use the equipment – was this an easy skill to learn or did it take time to master?

Key term

Interaction – when sports performers communicate effectively with the aim of attaining a joint goal.

Tactical demands of sport

Introduction

Tactics are required in all sports. The desired goal in sport is for the sports performer to win. When you think about tactics you will often think about team sports and set plays. However, tactics can be applied to individual sports as well. Whenever you have to make a decision in sport, you are applying a tactic. It is very important that sports performers make the correct decisions at the crucial points within their performance. This could be the difference between a gold medal and a silver in some instances.

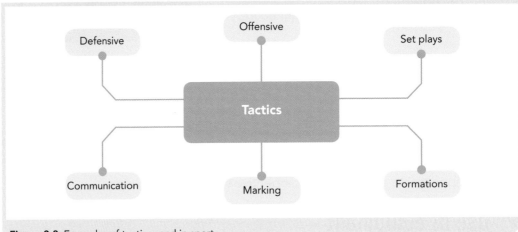

Figure 2.8 Examples of tactics used in sport

Decision making

After skills have been developed it is important that sports performers apply these skills correctly and strategically in competitive situations.

When competing in any sport it is important that a performer makes the correct decisions throughout the game, match or competition. The more you participate within your selected sport the more effective you should be at making correct decisions. For example, a netball player must choose the right player to pass to so that the team maintain possession of the ball.

Decisions within a competitive situation can often mean the difference between winning and losing.

Defending and attacking

Within all sports there are a great many strategies and tactics which are applied to defending and attacking. Particularly within **invasion games** like lacrosse and handball, strategies are applied to gain an advantage over the opposing team.

Key terms

Tactics – strategies or actions planned to achieve a desired goal.

Invasion games – a game in which teams have to get into their opponents' area in order to score.

Choice and use of shots or strokes

It is important that sports performers make the correct decisions to give themselves every opportunity to succeed.

Variation

In most sports it is important that the performers vary the strategies, tactics and skills that are applied within competitive situations, to avoid becoming predictable.

If a tennis player always plays a drop shot in the third shot of every rally, their opponent will start to predict the shot and react more effectively, thereby gaining an advantage.

Conditions

It may be relevant to apply different strategies within different situations in an attempt to gain an advantage over opponents.

In football, if a team is losing by one goal with only minutes to go and they win an attacking corner, they may make a decision to send the goalkeeper into the attacking penalty box in an attempt to increase their chances of scoring a goal.

Use of space

In many sports, the ability to create and find space provides a performer or team with a tactical advantage over their opponents.

In rugby if a team can pass the ball quickly out to the wing and create an overlap, space will be created for a winger (one of the quicker, more agile players on the team) to exploit and either gain yards or score a try.

A golfer must select the correct clubs to ensure that the next shot gets as close to the hole as possible.

| Activity 2.8 | Thinking about tactics |

Tactics can take many different forms. For each of the following situations describe the strategies and tactics you would use in an attempt to gain an advantage over your opponents within your sport:

- attacking
- defending
- when it looks as if you are going to lose but have a chance of victory
- when you feel as if you have no chance of winning at all.

Safe and appropriate participation

Getting started

Discuss in small groups the difference between isolated practices, conditioned games and competitive situations. Can you think of times when you have been involved in each situation?

Key terms

Isolated practices – training drills and skill-specific exercises.

Component – a part of something.

Introduction

When developing skills, techniques and tactics within sports it is important that this is done in a safe and appropriate manner, controlled and delivered at a pace which will support learning. By practising skills, techniques and tactics in a safe and controlled environment in isolated practices, technical errors can be highlighted and corrected by coaches before participants are required to apply these skills, techniques and tactics within competitive situations.

Relevant skills and techniques

Each sport has specific skills and techniques that are required for effective participation within that sport. In some instances, skills appropriate for one player's role in a sport are not the same as those for another player. For example, in order to be an effective batter in rounders the skills required are different from those required to be an effective fielder.

Relevant tactics

It is important that a sports performer or team apply relevant and appropriate tactics when participating in their sport, given any particular settings or situations. Tactics may depend upon a variety of factors, including:

- the weather
- the score/position the performer is in
- the time/distance left
- the opponent's weaknesses
- the performer's weaknesses
- injuries, if a substitute is replacing original opponents
- the opponent's tactics.

Effective use of skills and techniques, and the correct application of each

When using any skill it is important that this is done in a technically correct way, to ensure efficiency and effectiveness.

In order to consider the correct application of a skill the sports performer must consider the position that each part of the body should be in during each stage of the skill.

Through detailed analysis, elite sports performers have developed every **component** of each specific skill, which has resulted in improvements to their overall performance.

Activity 2.9   Sport-specific skills

Look at Figure 2.9.

- Think of a skill from your own sport.
- Explain the correct technical application of each component for that particular skill.

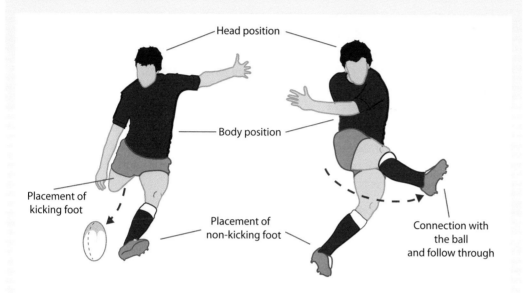

Figure 2.9 The components associated with taking a rugby conversion

Head position

Body position

Placement of kicking foot

Placement of non-kicking foot

Connection with the ball and follow through

Effective use of skills, techniques and tactics

Similar to the applications of skills and techniques, tactics also need to be applied correctly and at the appropriate time when you participate in **conditioned practices** and **competitive situations**. This ensures that they have the utmost effect on the outcome of the overall performance. For example, if marathon runners decide to break away from other athletes in a race too fast or too early, this may be at the cost of their own performance – they may become fatigued, resulting in them losing the race because of this poor application of tactics.

 Key terms

Conditioned practices – practices with special rules or restrictions that support the development of a skill, technique or tactic in a natural, game-like scenario.

Competitive situations – events or contests where more than one sports performer competes to achieve a set goal, following rules regulated by officials.

Assessment activity 2.2   2B.P4 | 2B.P5 | 2B.M2

You have been asked to produce a blog with video clips to support the promotion of sport within your local community. Select two sports of your choice.

- Produce written information for the blog about the technical and tactical demands of these two sports.
- Produce video clips to demonstrate the skills, techniques and tactics of the two sports in conditioned practices and competitive situations.

Tips

- You will need to give information about all of the skills and techniques required in each sport.
- Produce a voiceover for the video clips to discuss the skills, techniques and tactics that are being demonstrated.
- Remember your audience – you are promoting sport in your local community. Use your blog to give information about the skills involved in both sports, and how these skills can be developed for those who are new to the sports and are looking to find out more.

Observation checklist

In groups, discuss methods of effectively assessing a skill. Select a skill from a selected sport and observe a sports performer applying the skill, using a variety of methods of measuring success. Agree as a group on the most effective method of measuring success.

Introduction

An observation checklist is used by many sports coaches and sports performers to generate a picture of a performer's or team's overall performance. It is a tool to help a sports performer to assess their own strengths and weaknesses. The information obtained from the checklist can then be used to develop an action plan for development. It is important that before making decisions regarding such action plans sports performers discuss their findings with a coach or mentor.

Observation checklists should be used to prioritise the performance components for the future development of training programmes for performers, and they can also be used to monitor progress towards goals and targets.

The first requirement before completing an observation checklist is to identify the demands of a selected sport; often these can be divided into three areas of performance:

- **physical demands** (e.g. coordination, speed)
- **technical demands** (e.g. passing, serving)
- **tactical demands** (e.g. defending, attacking).

It is important that the performer has a clear understanding of the requirements for each component being observed and assessed within the checklist.

Table 2.3 An example of the components required for each area of performance for a netball player

Physical demands	Technical demands	Tactical demands
Aerobic endurance	Passing	Attacking
Speed	Receiving	Defending
Flexibility	Dodging	Creating space
Agility	Shooting	Positioning
Coordination	Blocking	
Reaction time	Intercepting	
	Rebounding	

Activity 2.10 Physical, technical and tactical demands

For your own sport, make a list of the required attributes to perform effectively under the following headings:

- physical components
- skills and technical components
- tactical components.

Shooting is one of the required skillls for netball.

Observing the full competition and then making an overall judgement for each component of performance after the event for the player/team is called performance profiling. When using this method, it is important to have a clear scale to indicate the levels of performance being measured. For example, if a 10-point scale is used, 1 on the scale may be unsuccessful application of the skill, technique or tactic, while 10 is faultless application of the skill, technique or tactic. Therefore if a performer scores 5, his application of the skill in question would be judged as having been average. Table 2.4 shows an example of a performance profile for a sprint start.

Table 2.4 Performance profile for sprint start

Performance Profile: Athletics Sprint Start	1	2	3	4	5	6	7	8	9	10
Athlete A										X

Alternatively, a tally chart can be completed for the full duration of the competition, identifying successful application of each component, and then drawing conclusions from the results obtained. Table 2.5 shows a performance profile completed in this way.

Table 2.5 A tally chart observation for a rugby match

Tally Chart – Rugby – Core Skill – TACKLING	
Number of successful tackles	|||| |||
Number of missed tackles	|||| |||| |||| ||||

What are the physical, technical and tactical demands of rugby?

Reviewing performance

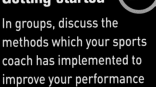

Key terms

Strengths – areas in which performance is consistently successful.

Areas for improvement – areas of performance which require development due to deficiencies in technique or application.

Video analysis – the process by which coaches and sports performers review video footage of practices and games to improve performance.

Introduction

Gathering information and making evaluations is the next process after the observation. The information collated by the observer must be interpreted to make judgements on the performer's **strengths** and **areas for improvement**.

Sport-specific strengths and areas for improvement

Skills and techniques

Through assessing performance, either by watching a live performance or through **video analysis**, an observer may notice that a sports performer is much better at applying some skills and techniques than others within specific situations. The observer should complete a summary of the performer's strengths and areas for improvement, providing possible reasons for each.

Tactics and effective decision-making

It is important that the observer examines the sports performer's application of tactics within a variety of situations, and analyses the performer's ability to make decisions under pressure. Feedback should be provided to the sports performer regarding their application of the tactics and strategies within conditioned practices and competitive situations as appropriate.

Activity 2.11   Team selection

When an international manager selects a team for a game, they have to consider the following factors:

- strengths and weaknesses of the opposing team
- strengths and weaknesses of the available squad
- having a balance of players

Work in groups to complete the following tasks:

1 Decide on a selection of players to play in the starting team of the next international match for a team sport of your choice. For each player, justify their selection.

2 Select the positions where each player will play. Justify your formation.

3 Decide on the specific tactics you would ask the team to apply, for both attacking and defending.

Non-sport-specific strengths and areas for improvement

Other areas for development may be highlighted which may not be specific to the sport, such as the components of fitness.

Activities to improve performance

After review, long- and short-term goals for technical and tactical development should be produced.

- **Short-term goals** are set over a short period of time, such as between matches or within a season.
- **Long-term goals** are set with the bigger picture in mind. Some long-term goals aim towards the next major competition, e.g. the next Olympics. These goals are often based around a training cycle or season.

Training programmes

Performance reviews should be used to create a training programme targeted to maintain strengths and improve areas for development. It is important to have clear goals in order to design a programme that is realistic and achievable.

Use of technology

Technology can be used to further assess performance, such as **dartfish technology** and **candlestick technology**. It is often used by elite sports performers to develop the finer details of technical application of skills.

Attending courses

In some instances it may be appropriate for performers to attend courses that support their own technical and tactical development. These courses could range from skills development sessions with coaches to coaching courses delivered by National Governing Bodies.

Where to seek help and advice

All of these performance development objectives should be negotiated with your coach/teacher, but be specific to you.

 Key terms

Dartfish technology – video software which shows a sports performance in slow motion, used by coaches to identify technical deficiencies.

Candlestick technology – video software which shows a sports performance in slow motion, used by coaches to identify technical deficiencies.

| **Assessment activity 2.3** | *English* | | 2C.P6 | 2C.P7 | 2C.M3 | 2C.D2 |

A coach from a local sports club has asked for your support. His club members are reluctant to take part in any form of self-analysis and rely heavily on the coaches within the club. The coach is a strong believer in self-analysis and would like to show the club members how this can be done.

1 Produce an observation checklist that could be used by sports performers to review their own performance. Do this for two sports of your choice.

2 The coach would then like you to show the club members how this checklist can be used:

- Review your own performance in each sport using the checklist.

- On completion of the review you should consider your strengths and areas where you can improve. Think of activities that will help you to improve your performance in the two sports.

- Prepare a presentation for the club to summarise your findings and how you went about this review.

Tips

- Before preparing an observation checklist, it is useful to first make a list of all the skills, techniques and tactics required to participate in that sport.

- If you have chosen the same sports as those you looked at in Assessment activity 2.2, you could carry out the analysis using the videos you made demonstrating skills, techniques and tactics for these sports.

Introduction

Have you ever thought about why some people seem larger than life when they play sport, but are really quiet and shy in everyday life? Or why some people stay focused and cope really well with pressure, but others crumble in high-pressure situations?

It is important for sports performers to develop ways of meeting mental demands in order to achieve sporting success, which involves training the mind as well as the body.

Those who work with sports performers, including sports coaches and sports psychologists, will need to understand factors that affect performance such as motivation, self-confidence and personality. No two athletes are the same so it is important to have a breadth of knowledge, understanding and skills.

This unit will help you to understand the different factors that can influence the mind in sporting situations and some of the ways you can improve your own preparation and performance, and that of others.

Assessment: You will be assessed by a series of assignments set by your teacher/tutor.

Learning aims

In this unit you will:

A investigate personality and its effect on sports performance
B explore the influence that motivation and self-confidence have on sports performance
C know about arousal and anxiety, and the effects they have on sports performance.

> This unit has really helped with my performance as a footballer. I understand now some of the reasons why I act the way I do when I play football and have been able to develop as a player as a result.
>
> Halima, *16-year-old female football player*

The Mind and Sports Performance

3

BTEC
Assessment Zone

This table shows what you must do in order to achieve a **Pass**, **Merit** or **Distinction** grade, and where you can find activities to help you.

Assessment criteria			
Level 1	**Level 2 Pass**	**Level 2 Merit**	**Level 2 Distinction**
Learning aim A: investigate personality and its effect on sports performance			
1A.1 Maths Outline personality and the effect it can have on sports performance	**2A.P1** Maths Using relevant examples, describe personality, including methods of measurement and three different views **See Assessment activity 3.1, page 85**	**2A.M1** Maths Explain three different views of personality, and how personality can affect sports performance **See Assessment activity 3.1, page 85**	**2A.D1** Maths Analyse three different views of personality, and how personality can affect sports performance **See Assessment activity 3.1, page 85**
Learning aim B: explore the influence that motivation and self-confidence have on sports performance			
1B.2 Describe types of motivation and the benefits motivation and self-confidence have on sports performance	**2B.P2** Describe types and views of motivation and the benefits motivation and self-confidence have on sports performance **See Assessment activity 3.2, page 97**	**2B.M2** Discuss the benefits motivation and self-confidence have on sports performance **See Assessment activity 3.2, page 97**	**2B.D2** Analyse the benefits motivation and self-confidence have on sports performance **See Assessment activity 3.2, page 97**
1B.3 Outline appropriate methods to increase self-confidence in sport	**2B.P3** Summarise, with relevant examples, methods to increase self-confidence in sport **See Assessment activity 3.2, page 97**		
1B.4 Outline factors that influence self-efficacy in sport	**2B.P4** Describe, using relevant examples, factors that influence self-efficacy in sport **See Assessment activity 3.2, page 97**		
1B.5 Outline goal setting, different types of goals that can be set and how these can influence sports performance	**2B.P5** Describe goal setting, different types of goals that can be set, and how these can influence sports performance and motivation **See Assessment activity 3.2, page 97**	**2B.M3** Discuss how goal setting can influence motivation and the roles of the different types of goals that can be set **See Assessment activity 3.2, page 97**	

Assessment criteria			
Level 1	Level 2 **Pass**	Level 2 **Merit**	Level 2 **Distinction**
Learning aim C: know about arousal and anxiety, and the effects they have on sports performance			
1C.6 Outline different types of anxiety	**2C.P6** Describe, using relevant examples, different types of anxiety **See Assessment activity 3.3, page 100**	**2C.M4** English Assess, using four theories, the effect arousal and anxiety have on sports performance and their control **See Assessment activity 3.3, page 100**	**2C.D3** English Evaluate imagery and relaxation techniques as methods of controlling arousal and anxiety, and in improving sports performance **See Assessment activity 3.3, page 100**
1C.7 English Describe, using two theories, the effect arousal and anxiety have on sports performance and their control	**2C.P7** English Describe, using four theories, the effect arousal and anxiety have on sports performance and their control **See Assessment activity 3.3, page 100**		

English / Opportunity to practise English skills

Maths / Opportunity to practise mathematical skills

How you will be assessed

This unit will be assessed though a series of assignments set by your teacher/tutor. You will be expected to show an understanding of personality and its effects on sports performance; of motivation and self-confidence and their influence on sports performance; and of the relationship between arousal, anxiety and performance. The tasks will be based on scenarios involving working in a sports setting. For example, you might be asked to imagine you are assisting a sports psychologist and have been asked to produce information to benefit different athletes.

Your assessment could take the form of:

- presentations
- leaflets
- posters.

Definition and structure of personality

Getting started

Think about famous sportspeople that you have watched. Do you think they act the same in their normal life as they do while playing sport? Why do you think there may be some differences?

Introduction

Have you ever sat down and thought about what your personality actually is? If you have, you will probably have described yourself using terms like 'bubbly', 'happy' or 'outgoing'. These are all terms that can be used to describe what makes up somebody's personality. You might also have found yourself thinking about how personality may differ from person to person, or in different situations. To be able to understand these things, you need to be able to define personality and understand the structure of personality.

Key terms

Personality – the sum of characteristics that make a person unique.

Discussion point

Discuss with a friend and try to come up with a list of words that you think best describe your personality. You may also want to start thinking about any differences that occur when you are taking part in sport, when you are hanging around with friends, or when you are spending time with your close family.

Mark Cavendish won Sports Personality of the Year 2011. What aspects of his personality helped him to achieve sporting success?

Definition of personality

Personality is the sum of the characteristics that make a person unique. People working within sport have long been interested in trying to find out just how much personality can influence sports performance. One way to start trying to answer this question is by looking at the structure of personality.

Structure of personality

Personality is a complex thing that is made up of lots of different levels. One way of understanding personality is by looking at it as three levels that are related to each other (see Figure 3.1):

- **Role-related behaviours** – this relates to changes in behaviour based on how you perceive the situation that you are in and your understanding that different situations require different roles. This is the most changeable part of your personality, because it is the one that is most closely linked to different environments. For example, a young rugby player may demonstrate more leadership qualities when captaining his rugby team than when he is sitting in a classroom doing his maths.
- **Typical responses** – this is the way that you usually respond in certain situations, for example, when somebody deliberately fouls you in a game. It is usually a good indicator of your psychological core.
- **Psychological core** – this represents the 'real you', rather than who you want people to believe you are. It contains your attitudes, your values, your interests and your beliefs. The psychological core is the most stable part of your personality and the most difficult part for people to get to know.

 Remember

Role-related behaviours and typical responses don't always truly reflect a person's psychological core because of how much they can be affected by different social situations.

 Key terms

Role-related behaviours – the least stable part of the personality, which is influenced by the environment.

Typical responses – the way that we usually respond to different situations.

Psychological core – the most stable and innermost, 'real' part of the personality.

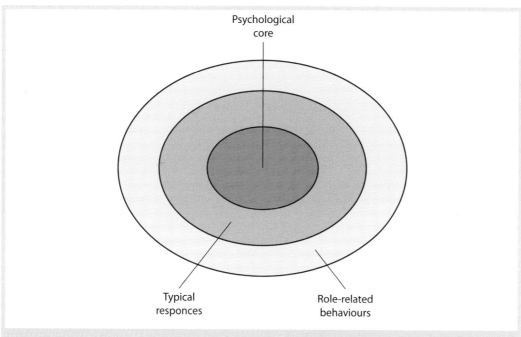

Figure 3.1 What does this diagram say about the structure of our personality?

Just checking

1 What is personality?
2 What is the structure of personality?

Personality types

Introduction

Have you ever heard athletes described as being aggressive, calm or a 'good leader', and ever wondered how those things may affect their sports performance? When people discuss these things, they are talking about personality type; the influence of the different personality types on sports performance has long been of interest to sports psychologists and coaches. In this section, you will learn about the different personality types, the differences between athletes and non-athletes and the difference between team and individual sport athletes.

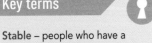

Individual sport athletes, such as long-distance runners, tend to be more introverted.

Key terms 🔑

Stable – people who have a relatively unchangeable mood and are not easily affected by their emotions.

Unstable – people who have a relatively changeable mood and are easily affected by their emotions.

◢ Personality types

There are four key personality types that you need to know about: **introvert**, **extrovert**, **type A** and **type B**.

Introvert

Introvert personality types tend not to actively seek excitement and prefer calm environments. Introverts also tend to prefer tasks that require lots of concentration.

Extrovert

Extrovert personality types can become bored with tasks quite quickly if the task requires lots of concentration and they have a tendency to seek change and excitement. Extroverts also tend to be able to cope with change better than introverts, and can cope with distractions like large crowds and lots of noise. Finally, extroverts also tend to be able to cope with pain better than introverts.

Type A

Type A personalities tend to work at a very fast pace and always need to be in control of situations. Unfortunately, this can lead to high levels of stress and can make them more susceptible to different cardiovascular diseases associated with stress.

Type B

Type B personalities tend to be less competitive and less concerned about things being done straight away. Type B personalities are also prepared to delegate jobs, are more tolerant and tend to experience lower levels of stress than type A personalities.

Other personality types

There are two other personality types that are important to know about – **stable** and **unstable**.

Effects of personality on sports performance

One of the things that a lot of people have tried to find out is the effect of personality on sports performance. To try to answer this, people have looked at the difference between athletes and non-athletes, and the difference between team and individual athletes.

Athletes and non-athletes

Some athletes have been found to have higher levels of independence, self-confidence and competitiveness, while also being more outgoing. Athletes also tend to suffer less anxiety (see Topic C.1) than non-athletes. However, the general conclusion is that there isn't a particular personality profile that will distinguish an athlete from a non-athlete.

Team versus individual sports

There are also some differences observed between athletes in different types of sports. For example, individual sport athletes, such as long-distance runners, tend to be more introverted, whereas team players, such as footballers, tend to be more extroverted.

To be able to understand the background to personality, you need to know the different methods of measuring personality (see Topic A.4).

Discussion point

Why could a personality type that makes you more tolerant to pain be a dangerous thing in competitive sport?

Remember

Some personality differences have been suggested between athletes and non-athletes but these differences are not well understood.

What personality type do you think Mo Farah has?

Measuring personality

Getting started

Why do you think it is important to measure an athlete's personality?

Introduction

So far, you have learned about the structure of personality and the different personality types. It is also important to understand how personality is measured. There are two main ways in which personality is measured: by using questionnaires and by conducting behavioural observations.

Questionnaires

Sometimes personality is measured by asking athletes to fill in questionnaires. Two popular questionnaires are Eysenck's Personality Inventory (EPI) and the Profile of Mood States (POMS).

Eysenck's Personality Inventory (EPI)

In Topic A.3, you learned about introvert, extrovert, stable and unstable personality types. The EPI is a questionnaire that helps you decide which of these personality types you fall into and measures your personality in two dimensions: introvert–extrovert and stable–unstable (see Figure 3.2). As these dimensions are independent of each other, you will get a personality result that combines both (e.g. unstable extrovert). It asks you to answer questions that require yes or no answers. Your score is calculated based on these answers and your personality type is suggested based on that score. Most people tend to score somewhere near the middle of the EPI.

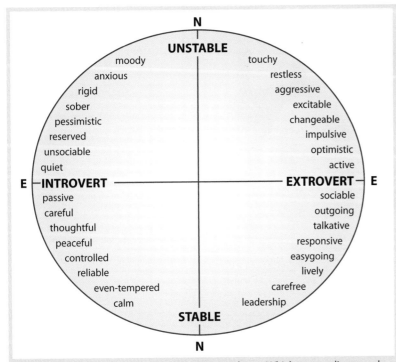

Figure 3.2 Look at the personality dimensions above. Which personality type do you think you would be if you completed the EPI?

Profile of Mood States (POMS)

The POMS questionnaire contains 65 questions and measures the following mood states: tension, depression, anger, vigour, fatigue and confusion. You are given a score for each mood state based on your responses to different statements (see Figure 3.3 for an example of the graph that is drawn from your results). For each statement, you say how you feel at that moment, or how you felt recently by choosing one of the following responses: 'not at all', 'a little', 'moderately', 'quite a lot' or 'extremely'.

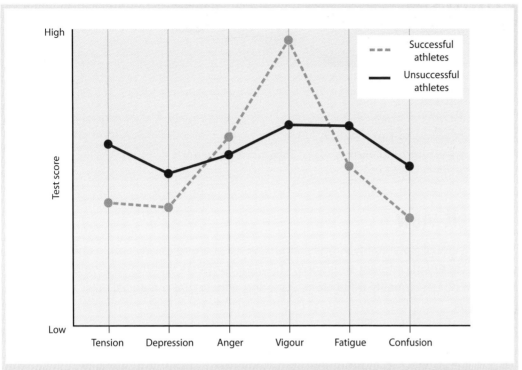

Figure 3.3 How does this POMS results graph show that mood state differs between successful and unsuccessful athletes?

Observations

Another way to measure personality is by **observing** people. When you observe people, you are looking for them to display particular **traits** or behaviours that will give you an insight into their personality. For example, when watching a football match, you may see the team captain regularly shouting out instructions, talking and listening to teammates and then always being the first person to do the television interviews after the games. From this, you might assume that the captain has high levels of leadership qualities, is quite outgoing and is quite talkative – all of which would suggest a stable extrovert (see Figure 3.2).

 Key terms

Observing – watching people to see which traits or behaviours they display.

Traits – personality characteristics that can be used to predict or understand behaviours in different settings.

Activity 3.1   Assessing personality

Watch a selection of different sports, pick an athlete to watch in each, and then answer the following questions:

- Which traits and behaviours do they display while they are performing?
- What do these traits/behaviours suggest about their personality type?

Just checking

1 What do the initials EPI stand for?
2 Which mood states does the POMS questionnaire measure?
3 What would you look for when conducting behavioural observations?

Views of personality

Getting started

Why do you think it is important for sports psychologists to understand the different views of personality?

Key terms

Views of personality – the explanations that have been given to help us understand why we behave in particular ways.

Trait view – the explanation that suggests our behaviour is based on personality traits.

Situational view – the explanation that suggests behaviour is shaped by our social environment.

Interactional view – the explanation that suggests behaviour is shaped by a combination of traits and the social environment.

Trigger – something that starts off a particular behaviour.

Introduction

The methods of studying and understanding personality in sport are known as the different **views of personality**. Three of the main views of personality are the **trait view**, the **situational view** and the **interactional view**.

Trait view

The trait view of personality suggests that our traits are relatively stable and consistent across a variety of different situations. This view suggests that the way we behave is based on our personality traits alone, ignoring effects that our social environment may have on us.

Not accepting the role of our social environment is a problem with this theory. For example, a boxer will get very aggressive in an important fight, but perhaps not in other settings. This suggests that the environment in which we find ourselves may influence the way that we behave.

How does Usain Bolt's personality differ on and off the track?

Situational view

The situational view of personality suggests that our behaviour is determined mainly by the environment in which we find ourselves and helps us to understand how a particular situation may **trigger** different behaviours.

This view explains behaviour using observational learning (seeing a behaviour such as a hard tackle in football) and reinforcement (seeing a significant other such as a coach or parent cheer on that hard tackle, even if it was a foul) to explain the influence of a situation.

A problem with this view is that different people will not react to the same situation in the same way, so their personality traits must have played a role in making them react differently.

Interactional view

The interactional view considers both your traits and the situation that you find yourself in when trying to explain behaviour.

A person with high levels of anger may not always display these in calm situations (for example, if their favourite rugby team is winning in an important game). However, if that same person's rugby team starts losing and an opposing fan starts to make offensive comments, then they could become angry and aggressive quite quickly.

What different views might there be on why a football player chooses to foul another player?

Assessment activity 3.1   *Maths*   2A.P1 | 2A.M1 | 2A.D1

You have applied for a work placement as an assistant to a sports psychologist who is working with a sports club. As part of the application process, you need to prepare a presentation to demonstrate your understanding of personality and how it can affect sports performance. You should use examples to support the points you are making.

Tips

- Make sure that you include a clear definition of personality and the different personality types.
- Remember to give information about the methods of measuring personality and a description of the views of personality.
- Explain how the different views of personality describe behaviour in sporting environments?
- Analyse the three different views of personality. Which view best explains behaviour in sporting environments? You will need to give your reasons.

Influence of motivation on sports performance

Introduction

Have you ever been frustrated by teammates who don't seem to be trying as hard as you? Their poor effort could be due to a lack of motivation. Understanding motivation can often be the key factor in being able to work well with clients as a sports coach or fitness instructor – it is an important part of getting the best out of people.

Definition of motivation

Motivation is the term we use to describe the internal mechanisms and external stimuli that arouse and direct our behaviour. This definition suggests that motivation is dependent on two sets of factors:

- factors from within us that influence our motivation.
- factors from outside of us, such as external pressures or rewards, that influence our motivation.

Our motivation will influence how hard we work towards a set task.

Types of motivation

There are two key types of motivation:

Intrinsic motivation

Intrinsic motivation comes from within you and has three key features:

- it comes from fun and enjoyment of the task itself
- it comes from personal satisfaction
- there is no external reward or pressure.

Extrinsic motivation

Extrinsic motivation comes from external sources and has the following features:

- it can come from rewards such as money, grades or trophies
- it can come from the threat of punishment
- it can come from the desire to win and beat others.

Activity 3.2 Understanding motivation

1 Working in a small group, discuss all of the reasons that you take part in your favourite sport or exercise activity.

2 Produce a spider diagram of all of the reasons that you come up with and say whether you think you are more extrinsically or intrinsically motivated.

Views of motivation

As with personality, there are different views of motivation that help us understand it. These views are the **trait-centred view**, the **situation-centred view** and the **interactional view**.

Trait-centred view

The trait-centred view suggests that motivation is created by our personality traits, our needs and our goals. When a coach refers to an athlete as a 'born winner', they are supporting the trait-centred view of motivation. A problem with this view is that it does not take into account the situational factors that can influence motivation.

Situation-centred view

The situation-centred view suggests that it is the situation that you are in and not your personality traits that will determine your motivation. A problem with this view is that it doesn't accept that your personality plays a role in shaping motivation, so this view struggles to explain how you stay motivated in situations that you don't like. For example, you may have played your favourite sport for a coach that you didn't like because you were determined not to give up.

Interactional view

The interactional view combines both the trait- and the situation-centred views to say that it is your personality and the situation that you find yourself in that will determine your motivation levels (see Figure 3.4). This view says that we have to think about how these two groups of factors interact if we are to best understand motivation.

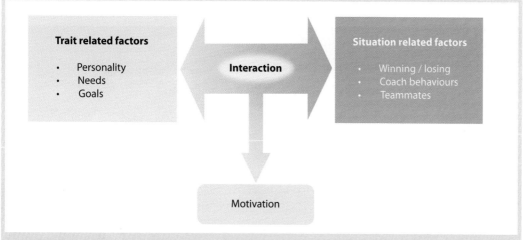

Figure 3.4 How does the interactional view of motivation help us to understand an athlete's motivation?

CONTINUED ▶▶

▶▶ CONTINUED

Key terms

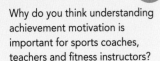

Achievement motivation – an individual's efforts to master a task, achieve excellence, overcome obstacles and perform better than others.

Motive to achieve – the part of achievement motivation that means that you will eagerly accept challenges and strive for success.

Motive to avoid failure – the part of achievement motivation that means you will worry about failing and avoid taking on challenges that may result in failure.

Discussion point

Why do you think understanding achievement motivation is important for sports coaches, teachers and fitness instructors?

Achievement motivation

Think about two football players. It is the last penalty in the UEFA Champions League final, the score is 4–4 and the opposition have just missed their last penalty. Which of the two players would take the penalty? The answer comes partly from a third type of motivation, known as **achievement motivation**.

Achievement motivation has two main components: the **motive to achieve** and the **motive to avoid failure**. In the penalty shoot-out example, the player who decides to take the penalty is determined to score and so has a high motive to achieve; whereas the player who thinks they will miss and decides against taking the penalty has a high motive to avoid failure.

Benefits of motivation on sports performance

So far you have learned about motivation, the different types of motivation and different views of where motivation comes from. Another important part of understanding motivation is knowing how it benefits sports performance. There are four key benefits of motivation on sports performance: choice of activity, effort to pursue goals, intensity of effort and persistence in adversity.

Choice of activity

Your motivation can determine who you choose to play against. For example, will you choose to play against people as good as you because they provide more of a challenge or will you prefer to play against people that you know you can beat because there is no risk of failure?

What types of motivation do you think are at work when an athlete makes an all-out effort for the line?

Effort to pursue goals

Motivation can increase your effort to pursue goals. This means that you are more likely to spend more time practising so that you can achieve your goals and become a better sports performer.

Intensity of effort

Your motivation can also affect the **intensity** of your effort. A more motivated person may train longer and harder in order to try to achieve a goal. If you are prepared to put more effort into practice, you are more likely to become a better athlete.

Persistence in adversity

When faced with **adversity**, people who have higher levels of motivation are more likely to keep trying so that they can experience success. For example, a basketball player with high levels of motivation is more likely to keep trying to play well even if their team is losing badly.

 Discussion point

Do you think it is possible to have too much motivation? How could this be a problem for athletes?

 Key terms

Intensity – how hard you are working.

Adversity – an unfavourable or negative experience that can happen during sport.

Why do you think that intensity of effort and persistence in the face of adversity are important to achieve goals?

Just checking

1 What is motivation?

2 What is intrinsic motivation?

3 What is extrinsic motivation?

Influence of goal setting on motivation and sports performance

Getting started

What do you think might be a problem with setting goals that are just general statements of intent? Do you think that they would have any positive influence on motivation?

Introduction

Have you ever set yourself the target of 'doing well' but then wondered what that actually means? Or have you ever had a target set for you and not known how you should try to achieve it? These problems are quite common and it is important to set effective goals so that you can get the greatest benefit from them. Understanding appropriate goal setting is important in lots of jobs, including sports coaching and fitness instructing.

Key terms

Goal – something that you want to achieve.

Barrier – something that could potentially stop you from achieving your goal if you do not work around it.

Link

This topic links to *Unit 5: Training for Personal Fitness.*

Principles of goal setting to increase and direct motivation

To set effective **goals**, you should remember the acronym 'SMARTER'. This stands for:

- **S**pecific – the goal must be clearly related to something you want to achieve, so rather than just saying, 'I want to get fit', you should say, 'I want to improve my speed.'
- **M**easurable – your goal must be produced so that you can monitor your progress towards it. For example, you could expand the specific statement by saying, 'I want to improve my speed by 0.3 seconds over 30m.'
- **A**chievable – it must be possible for you to achieve the goal.
- **R**ealistic – this links in with 'achievable', and takes into account any **barriers** that may prevent you from achieving your goal. For example, if you were injured, this would be a barrier to you achieving the speed-related goal mentioned before.
- **T**ime-related – there should be a timescale in which you will achieve your goal. For example, you could expand the goal by saying, 'I want to improve my speed by 0.3 seconds within 3 months of starting my training programme.' This provides you with a way to measure the goal.
- **E**xciting – the goal that you set should be challenging enough to motivate you to want to achieve it. So, for example, a sprinter who was told that they would be selected for a national squad if they could improve their sprint time by 0.3 seconds would be more likely to work towards the goal.
- **R**ecorded – have you ever heard the saying 'out of sight, out of mind'? The goal should be recorded in an appropriate way for the athlete and be kept somewhere visible. Progress towards the goal should also be recorded and placed on view.

Almost all athletes use formal goal setting as part of their training to improve performance.

Why do you think effective goal setting would be important for somebody like Wayne Rooney?

Remember

There is a relationship between motivation and sports performance. In order to perform well, athletes need to be motivated. As athletes improve their performance, they become more motivated to carry on improving.

Activity 3.3   Setting goals for yourself

For the sport that you play, set yourself three goals. Make sure that you apply the SMARTER principle so that your goals are effective.

CONTINUED ▶▶

Key terms

Outcome goals – these focus on the outcome of an event, such as winning a race.

Performance goals – these focus on the athlete developing their own performance, and allow the athlete to make comparisons with their own performance.

Process goals – these focus on what needs to be done to improve performance.

Goals

There are three main types of goals set in sport: **outcome goals**, **performance goals** and **process goals**.

Outcome goals

Outcome goals can benefit motivation when you are away from competition in the short term but can also decrease motivation in the long term if too much emphasis is placed on the outcome of an event.

Achieving this type of goal is partly dependent on your opponents. For example, if you are a 200m runner who has just started competing, you may run a personal best time every race, but are likely to lose if you are competing against more experienced runners. If your coach only focuses on the outcome of an event, you may get fed up because your personal improvement isn't being recognised.

How would you feel if you'd run your best time ever but came last against your opponents?

Performance goals

To attain performance goals, you compare yourself to your previous performances. These type of goals are normally more flexible than outcome goals. An example would be you saying that you wanted to improve your 200m personal best time by 0.5 seconds.

Process goals

Taking the 200m performance goal example, a coach may identify that the reason the personal best time is a little slower than expected is because the sprinter has got a slow push-off from the starting blocks. Therefore, the process goal might be to increase the speed and strength of push-off.

◤ Influence of goal setting on sports performance

There are lots of different ways that goal setting can benefit sports performance. The four main ways are:

What types of goals might a participant in your sport set themselves?

- **Directing attention to certain aspects of performance**: for example, a basketball player may set a goal to make sure they release the ball at the peak of a jump shot.
- **Mobilising effort**: for example, if a rugby player has put on weight during a period of injury, they may set a goal of losing 4kg prior to returning to competition. Once the goal is set, the player is likely to start to work towards achieving it.
- **Prolonging persistence**: for example, if the same rugby player is struggling with their weight loss programme because it sounds quite difficult, you can help to prolong their persistence by making the goal appear more manageable. The goal might be losing 0.5kg per week over 8 weeks rather than losing 4kg in one go.
- **Developing new strategies**: for example, the free-kick taker in football may find that they have increased their shooting accuracy, but to improve further (score more goals), they learn how to direct different types of free kick to different parts of the goal.

◤ Influence of goal setting on motivation

There is a relationship between improved performance and improved motivation. When a goal is set, the athlete's behaviour will be focused on achieving that goal. By monitoring and adjusting the goals, the athlete is likely to maintain focus on the task in hand, which can result in an increased performance. When an athlete improves their performance, they are likely to become more motivated as they wish to carry on improving.

Remember

The most effective way to use outcome, performance and process goals is to use a combination of them at the right times. For example, you may set a target of trying to win a 200m race (outcome goal) by improving your personal best time by 0.5 seconds (performance goal). To do this, you would need to improve the speed and strength at push-off from the blocks (process goal).

Activity 3.4	Setting goals for yourself

Looking at the goals you developed for Activity 3.3, make sure that they focus on a combination of outcome, performance and process goals.

Self-confidence and self-efficacy

Getting started

It is often said that to be a great athlete you must believe you are the best. What does this tell you about the effects of self-belief on performance?

Key term

Self-confidence – the belief that a desired behaviour can be performed.

Introduction

Have you ever heard athletes talk about having a strong belief in their capabilities, or believing in their teammates? Or how about walking into a competition, like a race or a game, taking one look at the opponents and thinking 'I've lost already'? These are factors that can be explained by understanding self-confidence and self-efficacy.

Definition of self-confidence

Self-confidence is the belief that a desired behaviour can be performed. It is one of the most important factors that separates highly successful athletes from less successful ones. The desired behaviour could be anything from taking a free throw in basketball to potting the black in snooker – the key part is your belief that you can do it.

Benefits of self-confidence

Athletes think self-confidence is important because it has lots of different benefits for performance. The main benefits are that it can produce positive emotions, improve performance, concentration and effort, and help you develop positive game plans.

Producing positive emotions

When you are more self-confident, you are more likely to remain calm and relaxed. You are also more likely to view symptoms of anxiety in a positive way and see them as beneficial for performance (see Topic C.3).

Improving concentration and effort

Self-confidence increases concentration because you are able to focus on the task in hand, rather than worrying about the negative parts of your performance. Also, when people believe that they are able to do something, they are likely to put more effort into achieving that goal.

Development of positive game plans

Athletes with high levels of self-confidence are likely to compete with the 'play to win' mentality.

Self-confidence often helps to focus sports performers before a competitive situation.

They are happy to make positive contributions and take responsibility, for example taking an important penalty in football. Athletes who have less self-confidence tend not to adopt this approach because they are worried about making mistakes.

Improving performance

There is a positive relationship between self-confidence and performance, but it is not completely clear why. Factors such as positive emotions, improved concentration and effort, and producing positive game plans have all been linked to explaining how self-confidence can improve performance. Every person has an optimal level of self-confidence but they can also sometimes become over-confident or lacking in confidence, both of which can negatively affect performance.

 # Methods to increase self-confidence

An important skill for people working with athletes is to help them build self-confidence. Two ways that this can be done are through **self-talk** and **imagery**.

Self-talk

Self-talk is a method of improving self-confidence. It works by athletes talking to themselves in a positive way, telling themselves that they will be successful. Positive statements like 'keep calm, keep focused and I can beat them' can help improve self-confidence as they help to remove negative thoughts. Simple positive statements that focus on an athlete's strengths tend to be most effective. You could try using the following types of statements:

- **emotional**: positive statements that can produce excitement
- **technical**: positive statements that focus on successfully performing a skill
- **memory**: positive statements that remind you of when you have done something successfully in the past.

Imagery

Imagery can help to improve self-confidence by providing you with an opportunity to picture yourself doing things that you have not previously been able to do or find difficult to do. It can also help you re-create a time when you have been successful and confident, and remind you of the fact that you are able to perform a particular task. For example, if you are a centre in netball and have suffered a badly injured ankle, as part of your injury rehabilitation you could picture yourself successfully pivoting on your injured ankle to increase your self-confidence in your ability to move, twist and change direction quickly.

> ### Key terms
>
> **Self-talk** – a technique used to improve self-confidence by telling yourself that you will be successful.
>
> **Imagery** – a technique used to enhance self-confidence by picturing yourself being successful.

Discussion point

Using the descriptions of the different types of self-talk statements, try to produce one example of each type of statement that you could use in competition and/or training.

Activity 3.5   Inspirational quotes

1 Research different inspirational quotes from famous athletes such as Michael Jordan, Bradley Wiggins and Tiger Woods.

2 Make a poster that shows a variety of quotations and explain what these athletes thought about the importance of self-confidence based on what they said in their quotation.

CONTINUED ▶▶

▶▶ CONTINUED

Definition of self-efficacy

Self-efficacy is self-confidence in a specific situation, and is related to being able to perform a task with a specific goal in mind. For example, self-efficacy not only means stepping up and attempting a penalty in football, but also firmly believing that you will score.

Factors affecting self-efficacy

There are four key factors that can affect your self-efficacy, and ultimately your performance: **performance accomplishments**, **vicarious experiences**, **verbal persuasion** and **imaginal experiences**.

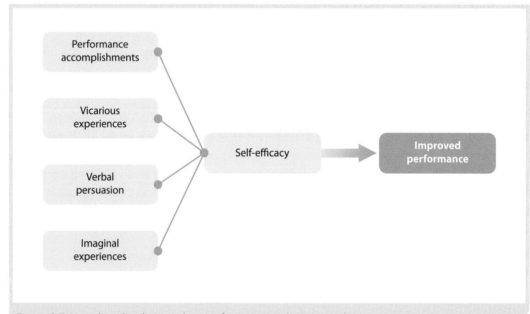

Figure 3.5 How does this diagram show performance can be improved?

Performance accomplishments

Performance accomplishments are one of the strongest factors that can affect self-efficacy. If you have a lot of accomplishments, your self-efficacy is likely to improve, but if you have experienced failure regularly, your self-efficacy is likely to be reduced.

Imaginal experiences

Have you ever sat and pictured yourself scoring the perfect goal, running the perfect race or hitting the perfect serve? Picturing this type of performance is known as imaginal experience and has been shown to increase self-efficacy.

Vicarious experiences

Have you ever watched a friend playing sport and thought 'If they can do it, so can I'? Vicarious experiences use modelling and demonstration to enhance self-efficacy. Seeing someone else perform well (particularly somebody of a similar level to you) will help to enhance your own self-efficacy, which can lead to improved performance.

Verbal persuasion

Has a coach or teacher ever said to you, 'I know you can do this, so just keep going'? This is a technique known as verbal persuasion and is important for developing self-efficacy. By knowing that other people have confidence in your ability to do something and be successful at it, you are more likely to start believing it yourself.

The best coaches are able to use verbal persuasion to inspire and motivate those they are coaching.

Discussion point

In groups, discuss the factors affecting self-efficacy that you have come across in your experience. Which did you find most useful for increasing your self-confidence and motivation?

Assessment activity 3.2   2B.P2 | 2B.P3 | 2B.P4 | 2B.P5 | 2B.M2 | 2B.M3 | 2B.D2

You have successfully made it through the first stage of the application process for a work placement as an assistant to a sports psychologist who is working with a sports club. You have now been asked to produce an information leaflet about motivation and self-confidence for young athletes as part of the second stage. This should include the following information:

- the types and views of motivation
- the benefits that motivation and self-confidence have in relation to sports performance
- factors that influence self-efficacy in sport
- the different types of goals that sports performers can set for themselves, and how these can influence performance and motivation.

Tips

- You will need to include sport-based examples to demonstrate your points.
- Make sure that you include all of the self-confidence and motivational factors that can enhance sports performance and say how they can improve performance.
- Consider how goal setting and outcome, performance and process goals can be used both together and separately to enhance motivation.
- Draw all of these points together by looking at the benefits motivation and self-confidence have on sports performance.

Know about the effects of anxiety and arousal on sports performance

Getting started

Can you think of a time when you have been getting ready to play sport and your heart started racing, and you started to sweat? These are signs of anxiety and arousal.

Introduction

Understanding anxiety and arousal, their relationship with sports performance and the different ways they can be controlled is essential to the work of sports coaches and sports psychologists when trying to improve an athlete's performance.

Definition of anxiety

Anxiety is the level of worry or nervousness an individual experiences.

Types of anxiety

There are four main types of anxiety:

State anxiety

State anxiety is a constantly changing mood state. It is the anxiety that happens when you find yourself in different situations. This type of anxiety is temporary and involves feelings of tension and apprehension due to the nervous system becoming activated.

Trait anxiety

Trait anxiety is a personality characteristic. It involves stable, consistent feelings of tension and apprehension across many different situations due to the nervous system being continually activated.

What types of anxiety might runners in the starting blocks experience?

Somatic anxiety

Somatic anxiety relates to the physical effects of anxiety. Some examples of this type of anxiety are butterflies in the stomach, increased muscle tension, increased heart rate and increased breathing rate.

Cognitive anxiety

Cognitive anxiety refers to the mental effects of anxiety. Examples of this type of anxiety are an increased feeling of worry, being unable to concentrate and being quick-tempered.

How arousal and anxiety affect sports performance

Drive theory

The drive theory says that as your arousal levels go up, so will your performance levels. A problem with this theory is that there are lots of athletes who report playing badly when they felt too anxious or over-aroused.

Inverted-U hypothesis

The inverted-U hypothesis tells us that arousal will benefit performance up to an optimal point, but before or after that point, performance will be lower. Most people can relate to this theory, but a problem is that it assumes everybody has the same optimal point of arousal and that everybody's performance will gradually get worse after this optimal point. This is a problem because different people have different optimal levels of arousal and sometimes performance won't decrease steadily – it will get worse really quickly.

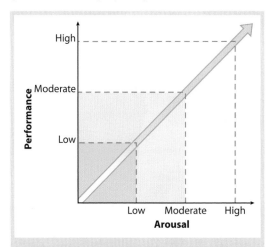

Figure 3.6 How does the drive theory explain the relationship between arousal and performance?

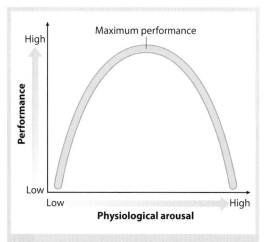

Figure 3.7 How does the inverted-U theory explain the relationship between arousal and performance?

Remember

During sport, you could experience lots of changes in anxiety types. For example, at the start of a tennis match, you may feel your heart rate increase (increased somatic anxiety) and you may start to worry about your opponent (increased cognitive anxiety). When you settle into the game, these levels may decrease but could then increase again if something important happens, such as the final set going to a tie-break.

Catastrophe theory

The catastrophe theory is a more recent development of the inverted-U hypothesis that says performance won't necessarily decrease steadily after the optimal point of arousal and that any further increases in arousal will lead to a dramatic decline in performance. This theory tells us that this dramatic decline in performance will occur if high arousal levels are accompanied by high levels of cognitive anxiety.

Reversal theory

The reversal theory says that it is the individual's interpretation of arousal that can influence performance. If an athlete interprets their arousal as pleasant excitement rather than unpleasant anxiety, they are more likely to perform well.

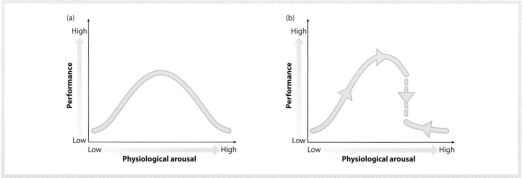

Figure 3.8 Catastrophe theory says that performance is affected by arousal in an inverted-U fashion only when an individual has low levels of anxiety.

Why do you think creating images in your mind, such as this one, helps people to relax?

How anxiety and arousal can be controlled

There are two main ways that arousal and anxiety can be controlled: through imagery and through relaxation techniques.

Imagery

Imagery can be used to increase and decrease arousal levels. You can decrease arousal levels by imagining a relaxing experience (such as walking on a beach) or rehearsing a successful performance (such as scoring a basket).

Relaxation techniques

Relaxation techniques such as progressive muscular relaxation (PMR) and breathing techniques can be used to control arousal levels. PMR can reduce arousal levels by enabling you to detect levels of tension in your muscles and then relax those muscles. Breathing control helps to reduce muscle tension, which benefits performance by improving coordination and skill execution.

What techniques might Jonny Wilkinson use to control his anxiety before a penalty kick?

Assessment activity 3.3   *English*   2C.P6 | 2C.P7 | 2C.M4 | 2C.D3

You have been asked to prepare a presentation for a group of young athletes to educate them on anxiety, the effects of arousal and the different ways of controlling anxiety. As part of your presentation, you need to include information about:

- different types of anxiety, using relevant examples of each
- the effects of arousal and anxiety on sports performance, using four theories
- imagery and relaxation techniques as methods of controlling arousal and anxiety, and improving sports performance.

Tips

- Give your views on which theories you believe accurately explain the relationship between arousal, anxiety and performance, which you think don't, and why.
- Consider each of the different methods to control arousal – which techniques would be most effective at controlling arousal, and why?

WorkSpace

◤ Samantha

19-year-old football coach

I really like my job. I get to coach football to all different age ranges and abilities, all of which present different challenges.

One of the biggest issues that I face is trying to get people to train outside when it is cold and wet. Trying to get them to concentrate on different areas for improvement is difficult when they just want to keep moving all the time if the weather is bad!

Another issue that I often come across is when players start to worry about the opposition, thinking that they might not be able to beat them because they might have lost to the same opposition before. It is really difficult for me as the coach if players go into a game already having lost in their minds.

One of the biggest benefits of understanding the mind and sports performance is knowing about different ways to motivate my players and different ways of helping them to cope with their performance-related worries.

Think about it

1   Why do you think it is important for sports coaches to have an understanding of the mind and sports performance?

2   How would the information on motivation benefit Samantha in her coaching role?

3   How would the information on arousal, anxiety and performance benefit Samantha in her coaching role?

4   Is this a job that you would be interested in, and if so, why?

Introduction

Have you ever thought about what happens to your body when you exercise? How does your body get to a point where it can run faster or longer or lift heavier weights?

As soon as you start to take part in any form of activity, such as walking to the shops, playing football or lifting weights, your body starts to respond so that you can perform that activity well. These responses will vary based on the activity and it is important that anybody advising individuals about the types of activities they are doing should be aware of these different responses. After taking part in regular activity, these responses will become long-term adaptations, and your body will change permanently if regular activity is maintained – for example, your muscles may get bigger or your heart stronger.

This unit will help you to understand how these different responses and adaptations occur in the body and prepare you for careers including fitness instructing and sports coaching.

Assessment: You will be assessed by a series of assignments set by your teacher/tutor.

Learning aims

In this unit you will:

A know about the short-term responses and long-term adaptations of the body systems to exercise

B know about the different energy systems used during sports performance.

When I went on work placement to a gym, this unit was really helpful because I could inform members about the benefits of different exercises. This made me feel more useful and they really appreciated my help.

Jamie, *16-year-old aspiring personal trainer*

The Sports Performer in Action

4

BTEC
Assessment Zone

This table shows you what you must do in order to achieve a **Pass**, **Merit** or **Distinction** grade, and where you can find activities to help you.

Assessment criteria			
Level 1	**Level 2 Pass**	**Level 2 Merit**	**Level 2 Distinction**
Learning aim A: know about the short-term responses and long-term adaptations of the body systems to exercise			
1A.1 Outline two ways in which the musculoskeletal system responds to short-term exercise	**2A.P1** Describe ways in which the musculoskeletal system responds to short-term exercise **See Assessment activity 4.1, page 121**	**2A.M1** Explain responses of the musculoskeletal system to short-term exercise **See Assessment activity 4.1, page 121**	**2A.D1** Maths Using three different sports activities, compare and contrast how the musculoskeletal and cardiorespiratory systems respond and adapt to exercise **See Assessment activity 4.1, page 121**
1A.2 Maths Outline ways in which the cardiorespiratory system responds to short-term exercise	**2A.P2** Maths Describe ways in which the cardiorespiratory system responds to short-term exercise **See Assessment activity 4.1, page 121**	**2A.M2** Maths Explain responses of the cardiorespiratory system to short-term exercise **See Assessment activity 4.1, page 121**	
1A.3 Summarise two long-term adaptations of the musculoskeletal system resulting from exercise	**2A.P3** Summarise, using relevant examples, long-term adaptations of the musculoskeletal system to exercise **See Assessment activity 4.1, page 121**	**2A.M3** Explain long-term adaptations of the musculoskeletal system to exercise **See Assessment activity 4.1, page 121**	
1A.4 Maths Summarise two long-term adaptations of the cardiorespiratory system resulting from exercise	**2A.P4** Maths Summarise, using relevant examples, long-term adaptations of the cardiorespiratory system to exercise **See Assessment activity 4.1, page 121**	**2A.M4** Maths Explain long-term adaptations of the cardiorespiratory system to exercise **See Assessment activity 4.1, page 121**	
Learning aim B: know about the different energy systems used during sports performance			
1B.5 Describe the two main energy systems, including examples of sports that use each system	**2B.P5** Describe the function of the three energy systems in the production and release of energy for sports performance **See Assessment activity 4.2, page 125**	**2B.M5** Using two selected sports, explain how the body uses both the anaerobic and aerobic energy systems **See Assessment activity 4.2, page 125**	**2B.D2** Compare and contrast how the energy systems are used in sports with different demands **See Assessment activity 4.2, page 125**

Maths Opportunity to practise mathematical skills

How you will be assessed

This unit will be assessed through a series of assignments set by your teacher/tutor. You will be expected to show an understanding of short-term responses and long-term adaptations of the body systems to exercise, and the different energy systems that are used during sports performance. The tasks will be based on scenarios involving work or activity in a sports setting. For example, you might be asked to imagine you are working in a leisure centre as an assistant fitness instructor and have been asked to produce posters to make customers more aware of the different benefits of exercise.

Your assessment could be in the form of:

- informative materials such as posters or leaflets
- presentations
- practical investigations.

Short-term effects of exercise on the musculoskeletal system

Getting started

Think about the last time you played your sport. What happened to your muscles while you were playing, straight after playing and then over the next couple of days?

Key terms

Musculoskeletal system – a combination of the muscular and skeletal systems.

Synovial fluid – a fluid that lubricates and nourishes a joint.

Cartilage – a tissue that protects the ends of bones.

Pliable – a muscle being able to stretch and change shape more easily without breaking.

Micro-tears – tiny tears in muscles that are necessary 'damage' for a muscle to get bigger and stronger.

Introduction

The **musculoskeletal system** is made up of your muscular system and your skeletal system. We use this term when describing how our muscles and bones work together when we are active. In this topic, you will learn about how the musculoskeletal system responds to exercise, including learning about **synovial fluid** production, increased range of movement, how muscles get bigger, how new bone is formed and increased metabolic activity.

Increased production of synovial fluid

Before we take part in exercise, we should always warm up. This prepares our body for exercise and means we are less likely to get injured. This is partly because as we mobilise our joints as part of a warm-up, more synovial fluid is released into the joint. As we exercise more, the synovial fluid warms and becomes thinner, easing joint movement.

Synovial joints also contain a layer of **cartilage** surrounding the bones which helps to protect the joint. Cartilage does not have a good blood supply, so cannot be nourished by the blood. When you exercise, your joint cartilage absorbs nourishment from the synovial fluid, helping provide the joint with extra protection.

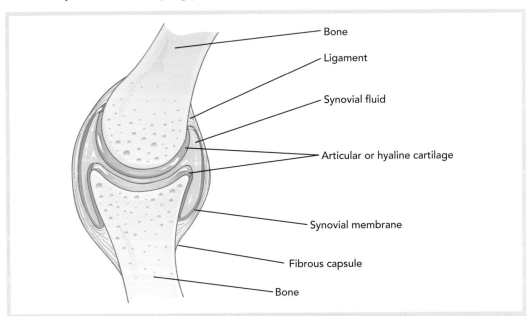

Figure 4.1 As we warm up, more synovial fluid is released into the joint to ease movement.

Increased range of movement in the joints

During exercise, our blood flow and muscle temperature start to increase. Our muscles get warmer because blood is being pumped to them at a faster rate. As the muscles warm, they become more **pliable**. This, combined with the increased level of synovial fluid in the joints means an increased range of movement.

Remember

Your body needs time to recover after exercise as this is when adaptations such as micro-tears in muscles being repaired take place. If you didn't rest, your micro-tears would not repair and may get bigger, which would eventually result in injury.

Micro-tears in muscle fibres

When you take part in resistance exercise, such as free weight training in a gym, this type of activity is designed to cause **micro-tears**, which are necessary breaks in the muscle that stimulate your body to rebuild the muscle bigger and stronger.

New bone formation

New bone is formed after it has been placed under stress. After a load, such as the additional weight experienced during a squat exercise, has been applied to the bone, bone cells travel to the stressed area and start to lay down new bone. The bone cells then produce and release proteins, mainly **collagen**, which is dropped in between the bone cells to increase bone strength in that area. Generally, people who take part in high-impact activity will form more new bone and it will be thicker and stronger.

Weight-bearing activities encourage the formation of new, stronger bone, which helps to decrease the risk of osteoporosis.

Key terms

Collagen – a protein that is important for bone formation.

Osteoporosis – a condition where you have brittle bones.

Metabolic activity – the body's way of releasing energy so that it can be used for exercise.

Enzymes – the catalyst for chemical reactions that release energy for exercise.

Take it further

Using the internet, research a disease called **osteoporosis**. How do you think that exercise can benefit osteoporosis sufferers?

Increased metabolic activity

Have you ever noticed that when you have trained for a long time you start to get hungrier? This is because exercise requires energy and your body needs to meet that energy demand, through **metabolic activity**. In order to maintain exercise, our body starts to produce and use more energy by using **enzymes** to start off chemical reactions that turn the food and drink that we consume into a useable form of energy. As well as providing energy, this process also produces a lot of heat, which can be useful when we exercise in cold conditions.

Short-term effects of exercise on the cardiorespiratory system

Getting started

When you exercise, you often turn red, your heart rate increases and you start to breath more heavily. Why do you think this is?

Introduction

The **cardiorespiratory system** is made up of the cardiovascular system and the respiratory system. You will often use this term when explaining how the body transports blood, provides oxygen to working muscles and removes waste products. Throughout this section, you will learn about important factors such as increased **heart rate**, increased breathing rate, how blood flow changes during exercise and how our body deals with increased build-up of carbon dioxide.

Key terms

Cardiorespiratory system – a combination of the cardiovascular and respiratory systems.

Heart rate – the number of times the heart beats per minute.

Anticipatory rise – an increase in your heart rate before you start exercising.

Adrenaline – a hormone that prepares your body for exercise.

Increased heart rate and blood flow

Before you start to exercise, your body experiences an **anticipatory rise**. This is because your body knows that you are about to start exercising and releases **adrenaline**, which increases heart rate to prepare you for exercise. As you start to exercise, your body releases more adrenaline to increase your heart rate further.

The blood is used to transport oxygen and nutrients, and remove waste products. Your increased heart rate is an important short-term response because the heart has to work harder during exercise to be able to supply enough blood to meet the demands of the exercise. Your body needs to be supplied with more nutrients and oxygen, as well as having waste products removed during exercise.

During exercise your heart and breathing rates increase so that more oxygen can be supplied to the muscles.

Activity 4.1   Effects of exercise on heart rate

1 Find a pulse point on your wrist; or if you have one, put on a heart rate monitor.

2 Sit in a relaxed state for 5 minutes and record your resting heart rate.

3 You are now going to take part in a stepping activity for 3 minutes. Before you begin, think about that activity for 1 minute. It may help if you are looking at the piece of equipment that you will be stepping on. Record your heart rate at the end of the minute.

4 Now complete your stepping activity at a fast, but not unsafe, pace. Record your heart rate after every minute of exercise.

5 Draw a graph of your heart rate from resting through to the final minute of exercise. What has happened to your heart rate at each stage and why?

Increased breathing rate

As well as increasing heart rate, your body also increases its breathing rate during exercise. This is so that more oxygen can be supplied to the working muscles and carbon dioxide can be removed.

Sweat production and skin reddening

Body temperature increases during exercise because of increased heat caused by metabolic activity (see Topic A.1) and other exercise-related factors, so your body needs to cool down.

As your body temperature rises during exercise, your sweat production increases. When sweat reaches the surface of your skin, it changes from a liquid to vapour and results in heat loss, which cools the body down. This process is known as **evaporation**.

Your skin goes red during exercise because the blood vessels in the skin dilate (known as **vasolidation**) allowing heat to escape from the blood to the skin's surface to cool the body down.

Redistribution of blood flow

During exercise, the body reduces the amount of blood to places where it is not required and sends it to other places that need more blood (see Table 4.1). This process happens when the arterioles that supply the less-active parts of the body, such as the liver and kidneys, narrow (a process known as **vasoconstriction**), while the arterioles that supply more active parts of your body, such as your muscles, vasodilate.

Table 4.1 Percentage blood flow in different areas of the body

Area of the body	Percentage blood flow at rest (approximate)	Percentage blood flow during exercise (approximate)
Skeletal muscles	15–20	80–88
Coronary vessels	5	4
Skin	10	2.5
Liver, kidneys, stomach, intestines	45–55	2.5
Brain	10–15	2.5–5

Key terms

Evaporation – change from liquid into vapour.

Vasodilation – widening of your arterioles.

Vasoconstriction – narrowing of your arterioles.

Did you know?

Evaporation accounts for about 80% of heat loss during exercise.

CONTINUED ▶▶

Lactic acid in the blood

Think about when you have been training or competing really hard, such as doing a heavy weights session or running a 400m sprint really fast. Remember that burning sensation in your arms or legs? That is caused by a build-up of **lactic acid**.

Lactic acid forms in your blood during **anaerobic exercise**. When you are low on oxygen or performing intense exercise and can't produce energy using oxygen, your body uses carbohydrates as a fuel source.

As carbohydrates are broken down into energy, lactic acid is produced in the muscles as a protective mechanism, causing your body to reduce your performance, by slowing you down when you are running, for instance. This allows you to recover and rebuild your oxygen stores.

After exercise, you should cool down so that excess lactic acid is removed. A cool down helps with this because it keeps blood vessels dilated, which means that lactic acid can be removed quickly. Having a sports massage after exercise can also help to remove lactic acid.

Cardiac output

An important short-term response to exercise is an increase in **cardiac output**.

Cardiac output is the amount of blood pumped per minute by the heart, and is important because it helps the body cope with the increased demands of exercise by transporting more oxygen and nutrients to the working muscles.

Cardiac output is the product of your heart rate and your **stroke volume**.

During exercise, there can be an increase of up to eight times resting cardiac output.

Your cardiac output can change depending on the types and levels of activity, gender and age.

Why do you think people might experience a high lactic acid build-up during intense work-outs?

Blood pressure

During exercise, your body has to work hard to deliver more oxygen and nutrients such as glucose to help you continue to exercise.

Blood pressure is the product of your cardiac output and the resistance to blood flow within the blood vessel. Therefore during exercise when cardiac output increases, so too does blood pressure.

Blood pressure has two parts; **systolic pressure** (when the heart pumps blood) and **diastolic pressure** (when the heart is relaxing and filling with blood).

Blood pressure is measured in millimetres of mercury (mmHg) and a healthy blood pressure value is 120/80mmHg. The first number relates to systolic pressure and the second number to diastolic pressure.

When taking part in aerobic activities such as marathon running that involve large muscle groups, your systolic blood pressure will increase because of the increased cardiac output, whereas your diastolic blood pressure will remain unchanged.

In contrast, during high-intensity anaerobic exercise such as weightlifting, both systolic and diastolic pressure will increase because your large muscle groups press against your blood vessels. The resistance to the flow of blood is increased, which increases total blood pressure.

> **Key terms**
>
> **Blood pressure** – the force exerted by blood against the walls of the blood vessels; the product of cardiac output and the resistance to blood flow.
>
> **Systolic pressure** – pressure that results when the heart contracts.
>
> **Diastolic pressure** – pressure that results when the heart relaxes and fills with blood.

What are the signs that this bodybuilder's blood pressure has increased?

CONTINUED ▶▶

◤ Increased tidal volume

Think about what happens to your breathing rate when you start exercising – why do you think it increases as exercise gets harder? It is because we need to increase the amount of air breathed in and out with each breath.

Tidal volume (TV) is the amount of air inhaled and exhaled during normal breathing. At rest, the average TV is about 500ml of air but this volume increases with exercise.

During exercise, there is an increase in muscular activity, which results in an increased amount of carbon dioxide in the muscles. When your body realises the amount of carbon dioxide is getting too high, your brain tells the muscles responsible for breathing to work harder so that you can remove the unwanted carbon dioxide quickly.

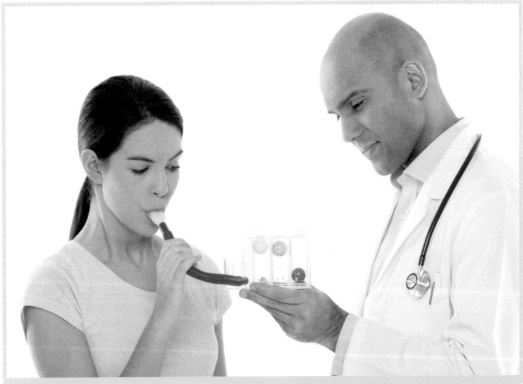

Tidal volume is easily measured with a spirometer.

Just checking

1 Why does the majority of blood flow to the muscles during exercise?
2 What is cardiac output and how does it change during exercise?
3 What do the terms 'systolic pressure' and 'diastolic pressure' mean?
4 What is tidal volume and why does it increase during exercise?

WorkSpace

▶ Emma

19-year-old fitness instructor

I work in a fitness centre that allows me to work with a range of clients – from older people and females who suffer from osteoporosis, to office workers who are sitting down all day so have terrible posture. I love the variety this brings me.

I get a different issue every day, which can be challenging at times and it is important that I know my stuff and can think on my feet. I also get to build a relationship with some of my long-term clients, which makes the job really fulfilling. I particularly like it when clients start to notice the benefits of their exercise, so that I can start talking to them about how much further they could progress if they keep going.

A typical day involves holding one-to-one sessions with clients, group-based sessions or sometimes team training sessions. It is really important for me to know not only what I am going to do with my clients during their session, but also to know why I am doing it by understanding the short-term responses and the long-term adaptations that result from exercise.

Think about it

1 How would the information on the short-term effects of exercise benefit Emma in her job role?

2 Why do you think it is important for Emma to know about each of the body systems when she is working with clients?

3 How do you think Emma would be able to tell if the fitness sessions she is doing with her clients are working? What adaptations would she look for?

4 Is this a job that you would be interested in, and if so, why?

Long-term adaptations of the musculoskeletal system

Introduction

When we talk about long-term adaptations to exercise, we mean changes that happen in your body after about 6–8 weeks of training. These happen because your body realises that exercise is harder than normal day-to-day activities, so it needs to make sure that it can cope with the increased demands. In this topic, you will learn about how your muscles, bones and joints change so your body can maintain participation in sport and exercise, as well as some of the general health-related benefits.

Long-term benefits for bones

Exercise has two main benefits for bones: increased **bone density** and a decreased risk of osteoporosis.

Bone density

As a result of long-term training, you will start to get an increase in bone density. This benefits the body because it means our bones get stronger, making it less likely that we will get injured if we fall over or take a bad tackle in football. Our bones get stronger due to increased **calcium** content. Table 4.2 shows some data relating to bone density in different types of athletes. Why do you think that the different groups of athletes have such different bone densities in the four different areas?

Why do you think volleyball players have a high hip bone density?

Table 4.2 Bone density differences due to playing sport

Sport	Bone density differences when compared to normal populations (percentage increase by body location)			
	Spine	Hip	Arm	Leg
Football	7	20	14	16
Weightlifting	12	6	20	11
Volleyball	12	17	6	12
Skating	5	4	5	5
Swimming	3	3	1	3
Gymnastics	12	24	7	10
Cycling	0	2	1	1
Running	0	10	0	10
Kayaking	0	0	10	0

Decreased risk of osteoporosis

Long-term exercise can reduce the risk of osteoporosis because it increases bone density, making the bones stronger and reducing the risk of fractures. Performing resistance, load-bearing exercise three to five times per week can reduce the risk of osteoporosis.

The University of Arizona has a useful acronym – **LIVE** – for remembering how to use exercise to benefit osteoporosis:

- **L**oad- or weight-bearing exercises make a difference to your bones.
- **I**ntensity builds stronger bones.
- **V**ary the types of exercise and your routine to keep interested.
- **E**njoy your exercises. Make exercise fun so you will continue into the future!

Link

This topic links to *Unit 5: Training for Personal Fitness.*

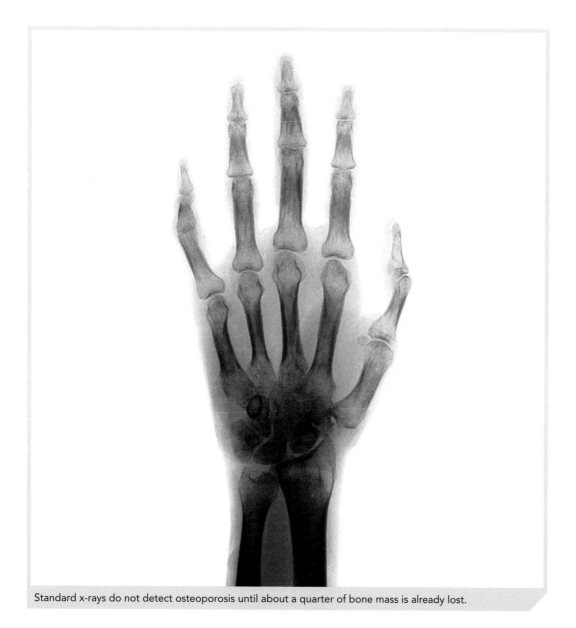

Standard x-rays do not detect osteoporosis until about a quarter of bone mass is already lost.

CONTINUED ▶▶

Long-term benefits for joints

These benefits include stronger connective tissues, increased cartilage thickness and increased stability of joints.

Connective tissues

Tendons and ligaments are made up of connective tissue. Exercise increases ligament and tendon strength because it causes them to stretch further than normal. This increases the number of collagen fibres in the connective tissues. This change means that you will be more resistant to injury for two reasons:

* you will have stronger connections between bones due to stronger ligaments
* you will have stronger connections between muscles and bones due to increased tendon strength.

Cartilage

Hyaline cartilage absorbs synovial fluid during exercise. Over time, by absorbing the nutrients from the synovial fluid, your cartilage becomes thicker and is able to protect the joints better.

Increased joint stability

Joint stability is how much your joints can withstand changes in body position without getting injured, and is an important part of all sports. For example, rugby players need to be able to change direction quickly without twisting or dislocating their ankles. Your joints become more stable because of the increased strength of tendons, ligaments and cartilage.

> **Take it further**
>
> Using the internet, research injuries in sports such as football, gymnastics and tennis and find out which types of injuries are most common. How do you think factors such as connective tissues, cartilage and increased joint stability can influence these common injuries?
>
> Some websites that may help include:
>
> * Physio Room
> * Gymnastics Rescue
>
> You can access these by going to Pearson Hotlinks (www.pearsonhotlinks.co.uk) and search for this BTEC Sport title.

A triple-jumper will benefit from increased joint protection and stability.

> **Key terms**
>
> **Hypertrophy** – an increase in the size of skeletal muscle.
>
> **Mitochondria** – the part of the muscle that produces energy aerobically.

> **Remember**
>
> Maintaining the correct diet and ensuring you have enough recovery time between training sessions are essential for hypertrophy to happen.

Long-term benefits for muscles

Long-term exercise has a number of benefits for muscles that can help you perform better in a range of sports. These benefits include muscle **hypertrophy**, increased number of **mitochondria**, the ability to use more oxygen, and improved posture.

Hypertrophy

Earlier in the unit, you learned about how exercise can result in micro-tears to the muscle and the body recognising this as a need to change (see Topic A.1). During your recovery periods, your body not only repairs the muscle fibres but also makes them bigger and stronger than before. This process is known as hypertrophy.

Regular endurance training will cause hypertrophy of slow-twitch muscle fibres, which will benefit performance in aerobic activities such as marathon running. Training that is more anaerobic, such as speed training or high-intensity resistance training, will cause hypertrophy of fast-twitch muscle fibres, which will increase performance in sports such as 100m sprint.

Mitochondria

Long-term endurance training can increase the size and number of mitochondria in a muscle. The size of the mitochondria can increase by up to 40%, while the number of mitochondria can increase by up to 100%. As mitochondria are responsible for aerobic energy production, this increase will benefit performance in sports such as marathon running, but will have little effect on sprinters or high jumpers.

Improved posture

Posture is affected over time by things such as slouching or leaning forwards over desks when working. These change the ways your **core muscles** work. The strength of these muscles plays a key role in the support and position of your spine. When these muscles are strengthened by long-term training, they support your spine and provide a more stable centre of gravity. These are essential for all sports techniques and can prevent some injuries.

Key terms

Posture – a position that the body can assume.

Core muscles – muscles, such as abdominals, that are responsible for maintaining good posture.

Did you know?

As a result of long-term training, muscles are more able to use oxygen; the muscles and their capillaries become more efficient and so you can exercise for longer periods of time.

Exercises that work your core muscles include bridges, planks, sit-ups and crunches.

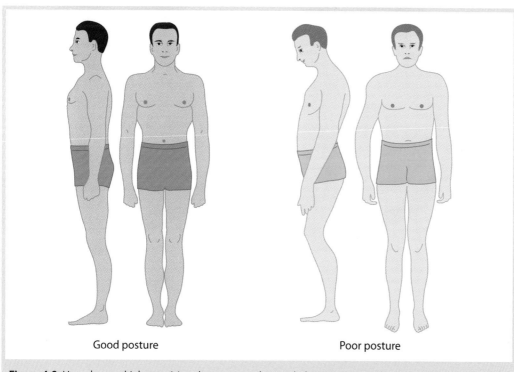

Good posture   Poor posture

Figure 4.2 How do you think exercising the core muscles can help maintain good posture?

Long-term adaptations of the cardiorespiratory system

Getting started

Think about when you have been training. Remember how it used to be quite difficult for you to run long distances, but now it is a lot easier? What has happened inside your body to allow you to improve performance?

Key terms

Gaseous exchange – the exchange of oxygen and carbon dioxide between the lungs and blood.

Cardiac hypertrophy – increasing size and strength of the heart muscle.

Bradycardia – a decreased resting heart rate.

Introduction

In this topic, you will learn about how long-term exercise can benefit your cardiorespiratory system. There are lots of benefits that increase health and sports performance, including changes to your heart, a decreased risk of hypertension, an increased vital capacity, increased maximum oxygen uptake and increased lung efficiency and gaseous exchange.

 ## Changes to your heart

As a result of long-term training, your heart increases in size and strength. This increase in size and strength of the muscles in the wall of the heart is known as **cardiac hypertrophy** (see Figure 4.3). Increasing the size and strength of the heart means that more blood can be pumped per beat, which results in an increased resting stroke volume and decreased resting heart rate. When your resting heart rate decreases to 60 beats per minute or less it is known as **bradycardia** and happens because the heart has become more efficient and does not need to beat as quickly for the body to be supplied with blood.

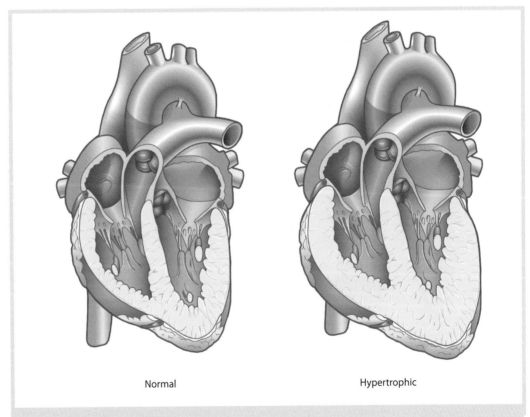

Normal

Hypertrophic

Figure 4.3 Why does cardiac hypertrophy lead to increased stroke volume?

Decreased risk of hypertension

A key health-related benefit of long-term training is a decreased risk of **hypertension**. This occurs partly because of the increased ability of blood vessels to vasoconstrict and vasodilate, but it is also partly because of an increase in **blood plasma** content. The increased ability to vasoconstrict and vasodilate means that blood vessels transport blood more efficiently, and the increased blood plasma volume makes the blood thinner. These two factors together mean that there is less resistance to blood flow, which decreases blood pressure.

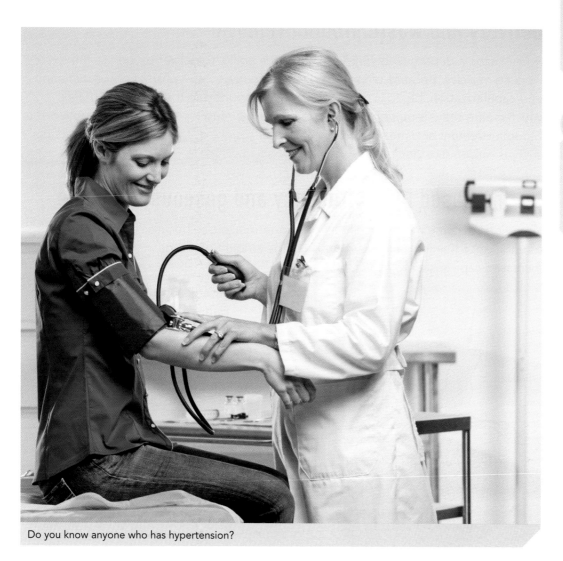

Do you know anyone who has hypertension?

Key terms

Hypertension – high blood pressure (greater than 140/90 mmHg).

Blood plasma – the water-based component of blood.

Vital capacity (VC) – the amount of air that you can forcibly expel from the lungs.

Did you know?

An estimated 970 million people worldwide suffer from hypertension, yet the risk of hypertension can be reduced by maintaining a healthy diet and being physically active.

Increased vital capacity

Vital capacity (VC) is the amount of air that you can forcibly expel from the lungs, and it increases as a result of long-term exercise. This increase is mainly due to the muscles that control your breathing becoming stronger, which means that your lungs can inflate and deflate more forcefully. This process helps the cardiovascular system to function more efficiently during sport.

CONTINUED ▶▶

Key terms

VO₂ max – the maximum amount of oxygen uptake, usually measured in ml of oxygen per kg of body mass per minute.

Capillarisation – new capillaries developing and existing capillaries becoming more efficient to help the movement of blood.

Increased maximal oxygen uptake (VO$_2$ max)

Your **VO$_2$ max** is your maximum ability to take in and use oxygen while exercising and increases as a result of long-term training. This is particularly important for sports such as marathon running, long-distance cycling and cross-country skiing. Two key factors that influence your VO$_2$ max values are the efficiency of delivering oxygen to the working muscles and the efficiency of gaseous exchange.

Increased efficiency of oxygen delivery and waste product removal

A key factor in determining your VO$_2$ max is the ability to deliver oxygen to the working muscles. Because of increased cardiac output, vasoconstriction, vasodilation and **capillarisation**, blood is more efficiently transported to the working muscles, which means there is more oxygen available for the muscles to use. This improved blood movement also means that it is easier for your body to remove waste products such as carbon dioxide.

Increased lung efficiency and gaseous exchange

Your lungs become more efficient after long-term exercise because activities such as endurance training cause an increase in the amount of alveoli in your lungs and increased capillarisation.

Alveoli and capillaries are key parts of the cardiorespiratory system because they extract oxygen from the air, transfer it to your blood and on to working muscles.

Alveoli and capillaries also remove carbon dioxide from blood and send it back out into the atmosphere. This process of 'swapping' the oxygen in air for the unwanted carbon dioxide in your body is known as gaseous exchange.

Figure 4.4 shows the process of gaseous exchange.

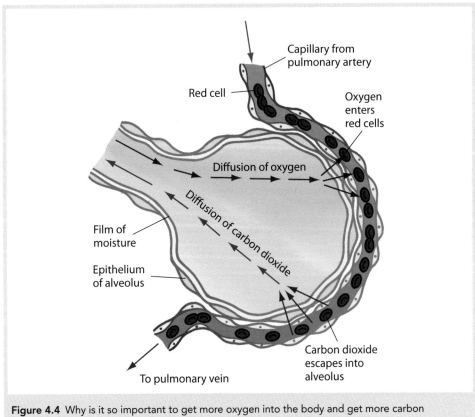

Figure 4.4 Why is it so important to get more oxygen into the body and get more carbon dioxide out?

A long-distance swimmer will benefit from an increased maximal oxygen uptake (VO_2 max).

Assessment activity 4.1   *Maths*   2A.P1 | 2A.P2 | 2A.P3 | 2A.P4 | 2A.M1 | 2A.M2 | 2A.M3 | 2A.M4 | 2A.D1

You have a part-time job at a leisure centre as an assistant fitness instructor. You have been asked to produce some educational materials that will make customers more aware of the different benefits of exercise. Produce posters that can be put up around the centre so the customers can read them at their leisure while using different facilities in the centre.

The posters should give information about responses of the musculoskeletal and cardiorespiratory systems to exercise, including:

- short-term responses
- long-term adaptations
- similarities and differences between the responses of these two systems, using three different sports activities as examples to demonstrate your points.

Tips

- Use results from practical activities to show the different ways these two systems respond.
- You will need to use relevant examples to describe the changes. For example 'In weightlifting, systolic blood pressure increases because ...'
- Give information about how the short-term responses and long-term adaptations occur. For example 'Mitochondria increases by ... this benefits performance because ...'
- When deciding which three sports activities to focus on, consider those which are widely contrasting. This will help you to make these clear comparisons. For example, 'In marathon running ... whereas, in sprinting ... sprinting is similar to weightlifting because ...'

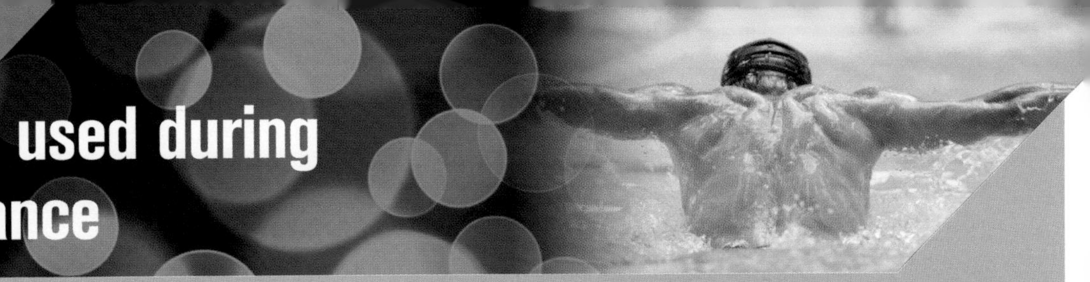

Energy systems used during sports performance

Getting started

Why do you think that a 100m sprinter would struggle to be able to complete a marathon? What do you think might be some of the signs that you are running out of energy?

Introduction

In these topics you will learn about how the body releases energy through **anaerobic** and **aerobic** systems to be able to take part in different types of activities. Understanding these different energy systems can be the key to structuring training programmes correctly or realising why you may get tired easily in different sports.

Key terms

Anaerobic – producing energy without being dependent on oxygen.

Aerobic – using oxygen to produce energy.

Adenosine triphosphate (ATP) – a molecule that is the only useable form of energy in your body.

Creatine phosphate (CP) – a molecule that can quickly be converted to ATP for energy.

Energy system – method of converting nutrients to energy.

Glycolysis – the process of converting glycogen/glucose to ATP for energy.

Glycogen – a form of carbohydrate stored in the liver and muscles.

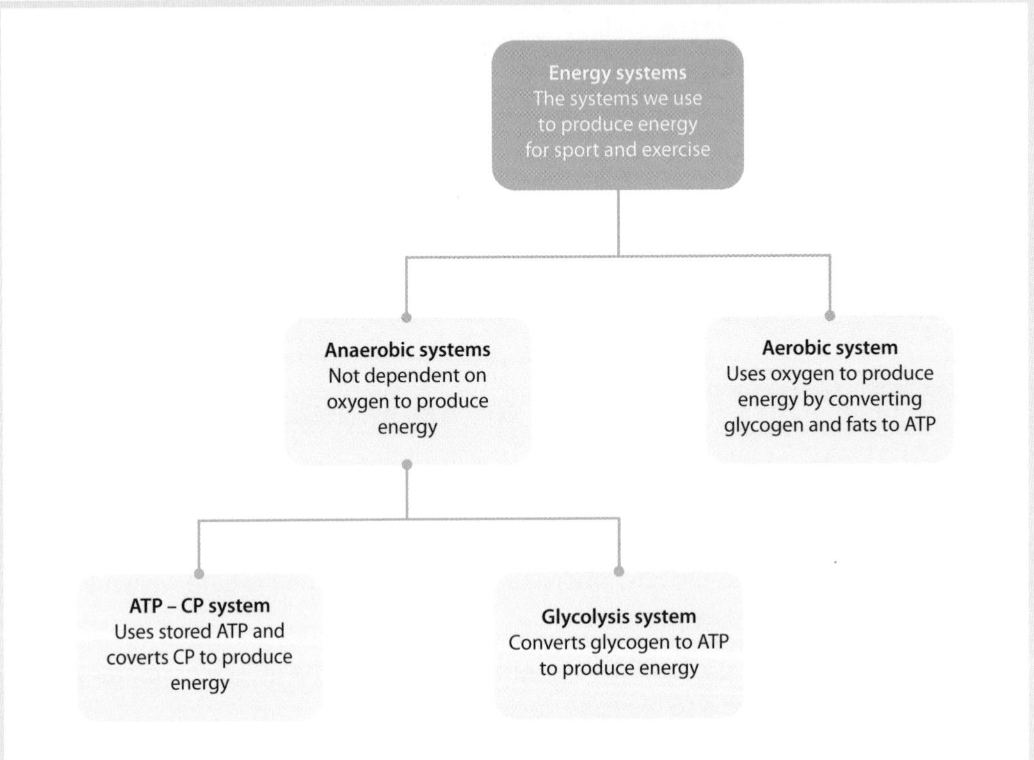

Figure 4.4 A summary of the different energy systems. Which sports do you think will be most reliant on each system?

The anaerobic energy system

This energy system is not dependent upon oxygen to produce energy and is used in sports that are high-intensity and of short duration. It is most commonly used for short bursts of activity lasting only a few seconds, such as sprinting, a shot put or the high jump.

Within the anaerobic energy systems there are two different pathways; the ATP–CP/alactic acid anaerobic system, and the glycolysis/lactic acid anaerobic system.

ATP–CP/alactic acid anaerobic system

This system has a reliance on stored **adenosine triphosphate (ATP)** to produce energy. The body has enough stored ATP to be able to sustain activity for approximately 4 seconds.

When stores of ATP run out, another molecule, **creatine phosphate (CP)**, is used to restore ATP levels. This is used because it can be quickly converted to ATP to provide the energy needed for short-duration, high-intensity exercise. The CP in your body is restored aerobically. There is enough ATP and CP combined in your body to produce energy for up to 20 seconds of activity, but often the stores will have run out after about 10 seconds. Therefore, this system is mainly used in sporting events such the long jump, 100m sprint or weightlifting. When the stores of ATP–CP have run out, the body uses a process of **glycolysis** to produce energy.

The Glycolysis/lactic acid anaerobic system is used in sporting events such as the 400m, 800m and 1500m sprint.

Glycolysis/lactic acid anaerobic energy system

Energy is produced using this system when the ATP–CP system cannot produce energy any more. This system uses glucose stored in the liver and muscles to produce energy. Your body gets this glucose from food and drink that are high in carbohydrates.

In this system, energy is supplied by a combination of stored ATP, CP and muscle **glycogen** from 20–45 seconds. After this time, energy is supplied by muscle glycogen alone for up to 240 seconds of activity, although this system does tend to reach its peak from 60–90 seconds. As energy is produced for this period of time and at a fast rate, sports that use this system mainly include the 400m, 800m or 1500m. Alongside glycolysis, there will be a large lactic acid build-up, which explains the burning sensation you will feel. This build-up stops any more glycogen from being broken down, so you then start to produce energy aerobically.

Take it further

Find out why carbohydrates are useful for many athletes. Think about the following two questions:

1 Where can you find the main sources of carbohydrates in your daily diet?
2 Why are sports drinks thought to be better for athletes than water?

Discussion point

Can you think of any other sports that this energy system would be important for?

Remember

Think of ATP as the only currency that your body can spend. Whenever you eat or drink anything, your body has to convert those things to ATP before it can use them for energy, just as when you go on holiday to Spain, you have to change your pounds to euros before you can buy anything.

CONTINUED ▶▶

The aerobic energy system

The aerobic energy system uses oxygen to keep producing ATP over a long period of time. This is important for providing energy for sustained activity in events such as marathon running, long-distance swimming and long-distance cycling.

As the glycolysis pathway only uses 5% of the available energy from glycogen, the aerobic pathway produces ATP from the other 95%. As well as energy being supplied by glycogen, this system also uses **fatty acids** to produce energy for 240–600 seconds of activity. The aerobic energy system uses oxygen to **re-synthesise** ATP and is the most important energy system for activities that are low to moderate intensity and last longer than 90 seconds.

The three energy systems do not just work on their own; during rest and all activities you will be using all of the energy systems (Figure 4.5 shows this in a graph), even if it is a tiny percentage (say 0.1%) of each. For example, during a marathon run, you would use the energy systems in the following way:

- ATP–CP system used to set off and run for the first couple of seconds up to about 10 seconds
- glycolysis used from approximately 10 seconds to approximately 3 minutes
- aerobic energy system used for the bulk of the race when you are running at a steady pace
- for the sprint finish, you will start producing energy anaerobically again because energy is needed at a faster rate than the aerobic system can manage.

Key terms

Fatty acids – produced from the breakdown of fat. Fatty acids are converted to ATP for energy.

Re-synthesise – to reproduce ATP.

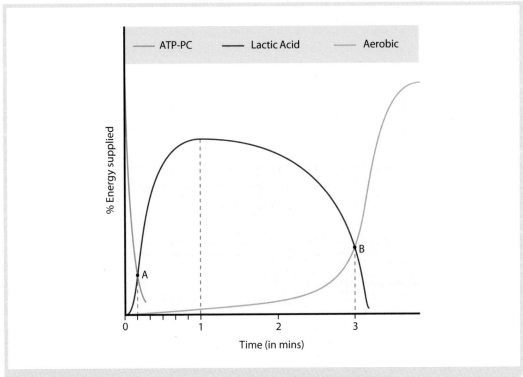

Figure 4.5 How does this graph suggest that the energy systems work together?

The aerobic system is important for providing energy during longer events such as long-distance cycling.

Assessment activity 4.2

While working at the leisure centre as an assistant fitness instructor, your manager asks you to deliver a presentation to some of the community-based athletes (three young sprinters and three young long-distance swimmers) about the different energy systems that are used during sports performance. Use sprinting and long-distance swimming as your example sports.

Tips

- When describing the different energy systems, you should include factors such as whether they use oxygen to produce energy, the length of time that they work for and how they produce ATP.
- What are the differences between these systems?

Just checking

1 Answer true or false to each of the following statements:
   a The anaerobic energy systems use oxygen to re-synthesise ATP.
   b The aerobic energy system uses oxygen to re-synthesise ATP.
   c We only use one energy system per sport.
   d The ATP–CP system uses creatine phosphate to restore ATP.
   e The glycolysis system uses fatty acids to restore ATP.
   f The aerobic system uses glycogen and CP to restore ATP.
   g The ATP–CP system is used in activities lasting longer than 90 seconds.
   h The glycolysis system peaks at about 20 seconds.

2 For any statements where you answered 'false', amend the statement using the correct answer.

Introduction

Have you ever wanted to start a training programme but didn't know where to begin? How do you train your body to the point where it can run faster, lift heavier weights or run for longer?

When you first start out training, you may find it a little bit daunting, but everybody starts somewhere. You will need to make sure that any training programme you design is specific to your needs and will allow you to improve different components of fitness to meet your goals. You will also need to make sure you are using training methods that you enjoy.

Whether you are training to become a high-level athlete or just want to be able to walk upstairs without getting out of breath, this unit is about understanding how to gather background information to help you design appropriate training programmes. It will also enable you to identify different barriers to training and how to overcome them before taking part in and reviewing a personal training programme.

Assessment: You will be assessed by a series of assignments set by your teacher/tutor.

Learning aims

In this unit you will:

A design a personal fitness training programme

B know about exercise adherence factors and strategies for continued training success

C implement a self-designed personal fitness training programme to achieve own goals and objectives

D review a personal fitness training programme.

I'm a competitive rugby player who plays for a Super League youth team, so getting a better understanding of training methods that can be used to benefit my sport was really useful for me.

Sam, *16-year-old aspiring rugby league player*

Training for
Personal Fitness

5

BTEC
Assessment Zone

This table shows you what you must do in order to achieve a **Pass**, **Merit** or **Distinction** grade, and where you can find activities to help you.

Assessment criteria			
Level 1	**Level 2 Pass**	**Level 2 Merit**	**Level 2 Distinction**
Learning aim A: design a personal fitness training programme			
1A.1 English Outline personal information for designing a fitness training programme	**2A.P1** English Summarise personal information for designing a fitness training programme **See Assessment activity 5.1, page 143**	**2A.M1** English Assess personal information for fitness training programme design **See Assessment activity 5.1, page 143**	
1A.2 English Design a safe four-week personal fitness training programme, with guidance	**2A.P2** English Independently design a safe six-week personal fitness training programme **See Assessment activity 5.1, page 143**	**2A.M2** English Design a safe six-week personal fitness training programme, showing creativity in the design **See Assessment activity 5.1, page 143**	**2A.D1** English Justify the training programme design, explaining links to personal information **See Assessment activity 5.1, page 143**
1A.3 Outline the importance of warm-up, cool down and FITT	**2A.P3** Maths Describe the principles of training and their application to the personal fitness training programme design **See Assessment activity 5.1, page 143**		
Learning aim B: know about exercise adherence factors and strategies for continued training success			
1B.4 Describe two personal exercise adherence factors and two strategies for training success	**2B.P4** Describe four personal exercise adherence factors and four strategies for training success **See Assessment activity 5.1, page 143**		
Learning aim C: implement a self-designed personal fitness training programme to achieve own goals and objectives			
1C.5 Maths English Safely implement, with guidance, a four-week personal fitness training programme, maintaining a training diary	**2C.P5** Maths English Safely implement a six-week personal fitness training programme, maintaining a training diary **See Assessment activity 5.2, page 147**	**2C.M3** Maths English Safely implement a successful six-week personal fitness training programme, maintaining a training diary summarising outcomes for each session **See Assessment activity 5.2, page 147**	**2C.D2** Maths English Safely implement a successful six-week personal fitness training programme, maintaining a training diary to evaluate performance and progress **See Assessment activity 5.2, page 147**

Assessment criteria			
Level 1	Level 2 **Pass**	Level 2 **Merit**	Level 2 **Distinction**
Learning aim D: review a personal fitness training programme			
1D.6	**2D.P6**	**2D.M4**	**2D.D3**
Review the four-week personal fitness training programme, identifying strengths and areas for improvement	Review the six-week personal fitness training programme, describing strengths and areas for improvement **See Assessment activity 5.2, page 147**	Explain strengths of the training programme and areas for improvement, providing recommendations for future training and performance **See Assessment activity 5.2, page 147**	Justify recommendations for future training and performance **See Assessment activity 5.2, page 147**

English Opportunity to practise English skills

Maths Opportunity to practise mathematical skills

How you will be assessed

This unit will be assessed through a series of assignments set by your teacher/tutor. You will be expected to show an understanding of training programme design and factors affecting exercise adherence, as well as being able to take part in and review a training programme. The tasks will be based on scenarios involving work or activity in a sports setting. For example, you might be asked to think about the barriers that could stop you from taking part in exercise and then come up with strategies to remove these barriers.

Your assessment could be in the form of:

- training programme plans
- practical observations of training
- training diaries.

Personal information to aid training programme design

Getting started

What personal information do you think you would need to collect to be able to effectively design a training programme?

Key terms

Aims – what you would like to achieve by the end of the training programme.

Objectives – how you plan to achieve your aims.

Did you know?

Over 50% of people who start a structured exercise programme drop out within 6 months.

Discussion point

Why do you think it is important to have lifestyle and physical activity information when you are planning a training programme?

Take it further

Visit the CESP website by going to Pearson Hotlinks (www.pearsonhotlinks.co.uk) and search for this BTEC Sport title. Then print off a copy of the PAR-Q form and follow the instructions to complete the form.

Introduction

When planning training programmes, you need to gather lots of personal information to ensure your training programme is effective; for example, there is no point including lots of long-distance running in a training programme if you want to improve speed and power.

Personal goals

Personal goals should be '**SMARTER**', which stands for specific, measureable, achievable, realistic, time-related, exciting and recorded. It is not enough to say, 'I want to get fitter', you need to make your goals much more focused. An example of a SMARTER goal could be 'I want to improve my leg strength by 20kg within 6 weeks.'

Goals can also be set over different timescales. These are known as:

- **short-term (ST) goals**: between 1 day and 1 month
- **medium-term (MT) goals**: to give progressive support towards achievement of long-term goals
- **long-term (LT) goals**: what you want to achieve in the long term.

Aims and objectives

The **aims** of your training programme are details of what you would like to achieve by the end of the programme. Your aims will be based on the goals you have set.

The **objectives** of your training programme are how you plan to achieve your aims.

Activity 5.1   Training aims

Think about the sport that you play or exercise activities that you take part in, and write down your training aims in relation to this sport or activity.

Lifestyle and physical activity history

When designing a training programme, you need to know about different lifestyle factors such as current physical activity levels (including physical activity, exercise and sport), alcohol intake, diet, free time, occupation, family and financial situation; all of these will influence how you design your training programme.

Medical history questionnaire

As well as understanding lifestyle and physical activity, medical history can also influence training programme design. You should complete a Physical Activity Readiness Questionnaire (PAR-Q) prior to training. This is a questionnaire that asks questions about medical factors such as joint pain, chest pains and dizziness.

As well as the questions on the PAR-Q, you may also need to give information about any medication that you are using. For example, if you have asthma, you need to make sure that you have your medication with you when you train.

Attitudes to training and personal motivation

Have you ever been getting ready to go to the gym and just thought to yourself 'I really can't be bothered'? This is a sign of a poor **attitude** towards training and a lack of motivation. Attitude and motivation are two factors that can affect your **intention** to train. This can in turn affect whether you decide to go training or not, and if you do, how hard you will try during your training session.

Key terms

Attitude – how positive or negative you generally feel about something.

Intention – planning to do something.

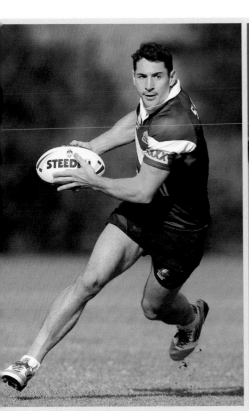

All sports performers must be motivated to train hard, play well and win sporting events.

Just checking

1 What do the terms 'aims' and 'objectives' mean?
2 Which lifestyle factors could you ask about when conducting a physical activity and lifestyle questionnaire?

The basic principles of training (FITT)

Link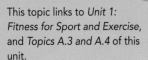

This topic links to *Unit 1: Fitness for Sport and Exercise*, and *Topics A.3 and A.4* of this unit.

Key term

Principles of training – factors that you must take into account to ensure that your training will be successful.

Introduction

The basic **principles of training** are those that you need to consider as a minimum when planning training sessions and programmes. These principles can be remembered using the acronym 'FITT', which stands for: Frequency, Intensity, Time, Type.

Frequency

The frequency of training refers to the number of training sessions per week that you will train. Novice trainers will usually start off training about three times per week, whereas experienced trainers or high-level athletes will train five or six times per week, and sometimes even twice in one day.

Intensity

The intensity of training refers to how hard your training will be. This is usually stated in terms of percentage **heart rate** or Rating of Perceived Exertion.

Time

The time spent training refers to how long you may spend exercising or how long training sessions will last for. You should make sure that you always think about the time of your training alongside the intensity of your training as they influence each other.

If you are doing some aerobic training at a moderate intensity, you would probably work for about 20–30 minutes continuously, but imagine what would happen if you tried to sprint as fast as you could for that long!

Type

The type of training refers to the method(s) (sometimes called modes) of training that you will use as part of the training programme.

If a sprinter was trying to increase the power in their legs in order to improve their sprint start, there would be little point in doing lots of long distance continuous running; they would be better suited to completing a plyometric training programme.

Can you think of specific types of training that would be useful when training for your favourite sport?

What principles of training do you use?

WorkSpace

Ritchie

19-year-old rugby coach

I have always wanted to be involved in sport in some way. When I was younger I thought I would be a professional rugby player but I got seriously injured in the first year of my contract and had to quit, so I then set my sights on becoming a coach.

To start myself off I enrolled on a BTEC First course at my local college and worked towards that qualification alongside doing my rugby coaching qualifications. I really enjoyed the course, particularly the units on fitness testing and training. These units gave me a much greater understanding of the importance of the fitness side of sports coaching, which has helped me to give more advice to the young players I work with. The course was particularly useful as I got to experience the whole process of planning, taking part in and reviewing my own fitness training programme.

Think about it

1. Which parts of this unit do you think would be useful for a sports coach?
2. How would completing this unit benefit young athletes who are developing in their sport?
3. Are there any other jobs that you think would benefit from the content of this unit?

Further principles of training and how they are applied to training methods

Link

This topic links to *Unit 1: Fitness for Sport and Exercise.*

Introduction

As well as the FITT principles, there are more advanced principles of training that you need to understand to be able to design training programmes effectively, to make sure that you are working at the correct level and will help prevent injuries.

Intensity

There are two main ways that you can monitor the intensity of your training programme: **heart rate** and **Rating of Perceived Exertion**.

Heart rate

When training, you can use target zones and training thresholds to select the correct intensity. This involves you calculating and applying your maximum heart rate (HRmax) to training. You calculate your HRmax by using the following equation: 220 − age. When training for cardiovascular health and fitness, 60% to 85% of your HRmax is the recommended training zone.

Rate of Perceived Exertion	Intensity
6	No exertion at all
7	Extremely light
8	
9	Very light
10	
11	
12	
13	Somewhat hard
14	
15	Hard (heavy)
16	
17	Very hard
18	
19	Extremely hard
20	Maximal exertion

Figure 5.1 The Borg (1970) Rating of Perceived Exertion (RPE) scale

Activity 5.2 Calculating HRmax

Using the equation 220 − age, calculate your HRmax. After you have done this, calculate your training zone for cardiovascular training by working out 60% to 85% of your HRmax.

Rating of Perceived Exertion

The Borg (1970) Rating of Perceived Exertion (RPE) scale is a measure of exercise intensity that runs from 6 to 20 (see Figure 5.1). It is designed to show people how hard they think they are working while exercising so that the intensity can be changed if necessary.

Relationship between HR and RPE

There is a relationship between RPE and HR, where RPE × 10 = HR (bpm).

Progressive overload

For your body to develop, the training needs to be demanding enough to cause it to adapt, helping to improve sports performance or overall health. You can overload the body by increasing the frequency, intensity or time of activity, or by reducing the recovery time. You should not alter all of these factors at once if you are a novice trainer because you will risk injury or developing a poor technique.

Specificity

When planning your training around the needs of your particular sport or activity, you should take into account the muscle groups used, the duration of the activity, the movement patterns and the energy systems used. You should set goals that are specific to the activity and components of fitness.

Individual differences/needs

Any training programme that you design should be specific to your needs. Everyone has different ability levels, goals, physical attributes, medical history and training activity preferences.

Variation

You should include a range of training methods to avoid boredom and maintain enjoyment. By doing this, you are more likely to stay motivated and adhere to your training programme.

Adaptation

An adaptation is where one or more of your physiological systems change as a result of long-term training. Your body notices that you need it to work harder when you are training and competing, so it reacts to the demands of the training and changes so that it can allow you to continue with training and competition in future.

Rest and recovery

Recovery time is essential in any training programme so that the body can recover from training and to allow adaptations to occur. Without this recovery time, the rate of progression will reduce and the risk of injury will increase.

Reversibility

If training stops or the intensity of training is too low to cause adaptation, the training effects are reversed.

Link

This topic links to *Unit 4: The Sports Performer in Action*. Refer to Unit 4 when you are learning about how the different physiological systems adapt to training.

Discussion point

Research the terms 'overuse injuries' and 'over training', and give an example of one. Discuss with friends how you think the correct use of the basic and further principles of training could prevent an overuse injury.

Just checking

Answer 'true' or 'false' to each of the following statements:

1 Specificity is making sure that you have enough recovery time in your training programme.

2 Variation helps to avoid boredom in training programmes by including a range of activities.

3 An adaptation is where the body reacts to a training load and changes to make sure that it can cope with training.

4 Progressive overload means that you gradually make things harder so that your body keeps adapting.

5 Rest and recovery is wasted time that could be spent training.

Programme design

Getting started

Why do you think it is important for fitness instructors and personal trainers to have a detailed knowledge of lots of different training methods?

Link

This topic links to *Unit 1: Fitness for Sport and Exercise.*

Introduction

There are lots of factors that you need to take into account when you are designing your training programme, including the selection of appropriate methods, safety in design, warm-up, cool down and maintaining adherence.

Selection of appropriate training methods

Speed and power training

Many sports require **speed** and **power** if you are to compete successfully. Although these are two different components of fitness, they do affect each other: for example, your power will determine how quickly you can accelerate to top speed. It is because of this that speed and power training are often combined.

Three common training methods to develop speed and power are **resisted sprints**, **plyometric training** and **speed ladder training**.

If you are planning to use speed and power training within a training session, it should take place after a warm-up or a low-intensity training method.

Resisted sprints are when you use equipment to make a sprint harder. By doing this, you make your muscles get used to sprinting against resistance so that when you stop using the equipment, you will be able to sprint faster because the extra weight is not there. These methods will often use distances of 10–200m depending on the sport. Examples of this type of training include parachute sprints and sled sprints.

Activity 5.3	Speed and power training

Using the internet, search for film clips of the different methods of speed and power training that are suited to your particular sport or activity.

Then use these along with information from the websites to plan a plyometric training session.

You may want to visit the following websites by going to Pearson Hotlinks (www.pearsonhotlinks.co.uk) and search for this BTEC Sport title.

- Live Strong
- Newitts
- Sports Fitness Advisor
- Strength Coach
- Youtube.

Speed ladder training involves people sprinting through the rungs of plastic ladders that are placed on the floor. It increases speed by forcing the feet to adapt to fast footwork patterns through repetition. You should begin with slow, controlled movements and progress to more advanced movements so that your muscle system can get used to the movement patterns.

How does plyometric training improve Andy Murray's power?

Plyometric training is regularly used to increase power in sports. Try to think of a muscle as an elastic band – the elastic band will fly further if you stretch it more before letting go. Plyometric training takes a muscle through an eccentric muscle action that lengthens and stretches it before a powerful concentric action. Over time, this makes for a faster rate of muscle contraction, which will improve power and speed.

Why is speed ladder training popular in sports such as football, rugby and basketball?

CONTINUED ▶▶

Flexibility training

Flexibility training works by stretching the muscles beyond their usual limits. As flexibility is affected by temperature, it is best to do this type of training after you have warmed the muscles up. There are three main types of flexibility training: **static stretching**, **dynamic stretching** and **Proprioceptive Neuromuscular Facilitation (PNF)**.

Static stretching uses slow, controlled movements to stretch a muscle and joint to its limit (see Figure 5.2 for examples of different static stretches). You can do this type of stretching on your own (active stretching) or you may be assisted by a partner, who stretches the area for you (passive stretching). This type of stretch can be held for up to 60 seconds.

Standing calf stretch   Pectoralis stretch   Quadriceps stretch

Standing hamstring stretch   Hip flexor stretch   Double knee to chest

Figure 5.2 Examples of different static stretches

Dynamic stretching involves performing activities that are similar to the sporting movements that will be needed during a game or event. For example, before games, you will see football players performing kicking movements without actually kicking the ball. This is a form of dynamic stretching.

PNF stretching is an effective form of passive stretching that involves three stages:

1 Stretch the targeted muscle group as far as it can go.

2 While in that position, **isometrically** contract the muscle group against a partner for 6 seconds.

3 Relax the muscle group and allow your partner to stretch it again. It should go further now.

Key term

Isometric – muscular action in which tension develops but there is no change in muscle length and no joint movement.

Discussion point

Why do you think you would have to be very careful when performing PNF stretching?

Muscular strength and endurance training

To improve muscular strength and endurance you will usually use the same training methods but will alter the **repetitions**, **sets** or frequency to suit either strength development or endurance development (see Table 5.1). The most common methods of improving muscular strength and endurance are:

- resistance machines
- free weights
- medicine ball training
- circuit training
- core stability training.

Key terms

Repetitions – the number of times you perform a single exercise such as a biceps curl; often abbreviated to 'reps'.

Sets – a group of repetitions; for example, an experienced strength trainer may complete three sets of six reps.

1-RM – the maximum amount of weight that you can lift in a single repetition. This is a measure often used to decide on the intensity of strength training programmes.

Table 5.1 Guidelines for strength and endurance training

Strength/ endurance	Intensity	Reps	Sets	Frequency	Length of programme
Inexperienced strength trainers	70–80% 1-RM or 8–12-RM	8–12	≥1	3	≥6 weeks
Experienced strength trainers	85–100% 1-RM or 1–6-RM	1–6	≥3	5–6	≥12 weeks
Muscle endurance	≤60% 1-RM or 15–20-RM	15–20	≥1	3	≥6 weeks

Circuit training is also a way of improving muscular strength and endurance. Circuit training uses a number of different stations that have exercises on them. The circuit can be designed so that exercises that use either body weight as resistance (for example, press-ups), or that use additional weight such as dumb-bells (for example, triceps extensions) can be included. You will usually exercise for about 1 minute per station and have a rest period in between stations. You can make your circuit easier or harder by changing the following:

- length of rest periods
- number of stations
- number of circuits
- time spent at each station.

Remember

When designing circuit training sessions, you should make sure that you do not work the same muscle group on consecutive stations to prevent fatigue.

CONTINUED ▶▶

Aerobic endurance training

The three main methods of training **aerobic endurance** are **continuous training**, **fartlek training** and **interval training**.

Continuous training is also known as steady-state or long, slow, distance training. It involves the athlete training at a moderate intensity over a long distance and time, usually by running, swimming or cycling. Due to the lower level of intensity, an athlete can train for longer. It can also be useful for beginners who are starting structured exercise, athletes recovering from injury and 'specific population' individuals such as children or elderly people. Some problems with this training method include a higher risk of injury when running long distances on hard surfaces; it can get boring and it is not always sport-specific.

Fartlek training is based on running outdoors, and varies the intensity of work according to the athlete's requirements. The simplest way of varying intensity is by alternating between walking, jogging, running and sprinting; the intensity can also be varied by running on different surfaces such as hills, soft grassland or woodland. Fartlek training can be more useful than continuous training because it can be made sport-specific. The variation it provides can also be used to make training more interesting.

Would you enjoy fartlek training more than continuous training or interval training?

In **interval training**, athletes perform a work period, followed by a rest or recovery period, before completing another work period. When designing interval training sessions, you should think about:

- the number of intervals (rest and work periods)
- the intensity of the work interval
- the duration of the work interval
- the duration of the rest interval
- the intensity of the rest interval.

An example of an interval training prescription for aerobic endurance could be one set of three repetitions of 5-minute runs alternated with 2 minutes and 30 seconds of rest.

Activity 5.6   Identifying training methods

Match the training method to the component of fitness:

Training method	Component of fitness
Plyometric training	Flexibility
PNF	Muscular strength/muscular endurance
Resisted sprints	Aerobic endurance
Continuous training	Speed and power
Free weight training	Aerobic endurance
Fartlek training	Speed and power

Safe design

In order to make sure that your training programme is safe, you should select appropriate training methods or an appropriate combination of training methods. These methods should allow you to meet your personal training needs, goals, aims and objectives.

Selection of appropriate activities for warm-up

When warming up, you should make sure that you use light, continuous physical activity to prepare the body for exercise. This will help prepare the body by increasing heart rate, increasing breathing rate and increasing muscle temperature. It could include activities like jogging, running in different directions and completing different sporting actions such as passing a rugby ball between teammates.

Selection of appropriate activities for cool down

In the same way that you need to warm up, you need to use similar activities to cool down. These activities will help you to reduce heart rate at a steady pace, which will help to remove lactic acid and prevent **blood pooling**. It could include activities like jogging or cycling.

Creative design

To creatively design your training programme, you need to think about how you can prevent **barriers** (see Topics B.1 and B.2) to ensure that **exercise adherence** is maintained and the programme is enjoyable. You could make the programme interesting by including a range of activities. This will help to maintain motivation and commitment as well as prevent boredom.

When you design a training programme you must think about your goals, aims and objectives.

Key terms

Blood pooling – the process whereby, when exercise is suddenly stopped, blood is no longer forced to return to the heart and so stays in the legs, which potentially causes pain and swelling.

Exercise adherence – how well you stick to your exercise programme.

Just checking

1 Name three ways of improving flexibility.

2 What are the three stages of PNF?

3 What do the terms 'repetitions' and 'sets' mean?

4 Name three methods of aerobic endurance training.

5 What factors can you change to make circuit training either easier or harder?

6 How does a warm-up prepare the body for exercise?

7 What are the benefits of cooling down?

Exercise adherence factors and strategies to overcome barriers

Introduction

There are lots of factors that can determine whether people will adhere to a training programme or not. It is important that you know about them so you can come up with strategies to overcome them.

Factors affecting exercise adherence

There are lots of reasons why people don't take part in enough exercise:

- **Access to facilities**: if people think they don't have access to facilities such as gyms and fitness centres, they are less likely to exercise.
- **Time**: quite often people who don't exercise will say that they don't have time to fit it into their daily routine.
- **Commitment**: sometimes people will think that they are likely to give up exercising so don't bother to start a training programme or drop out soon after starting.
- **Lack of interest**: some people just don't like the idea of exercise so choose not to take part.
- **Personal injury**: if people have been injured they may be scared of repeat injury.
- **Emotional**: some people can feel quite embarrassed when exercising, worrying about how they look and feeling that they cannot do it.
- **Cost**: people sometimes think that exercise comes with a lot of costs for things such as gym memberships and kit.

Would you feel confident training with these people?

Strategies to overcome barriers

There are many ways to overcome barriers to exercise.

SMARTER targets

By setting SMARTER targets and using rewards for achieving goals, you can help to improve commitment and motivation.

Implementing enjoyable activities

If you use activities that you enjoy as part of your training programme, it will become less of a chore and you will stay interested.

Training with others

Training with others can often provide the necessary support to motivate you to keep training. Reinforcement from friends that your training is having a positive impact will also help to motive you.

Knowing the benefits of training programmes

If you know the benefits of training programmes you are more likely to take part. For example, if you have been injured, understanding the benefits of training and the potential for rehabilitation could make you more confident.

Link

See *Topic A.1* for more information on SMARTER targets.

Remember

Rewards are good but don't rely on them; they should not be the only reason to take part in exercise.

Assessment activity 5.1   *Maths English*   2A.P1 | 2A.P2 | 2A.P3 | 2B.P4 | 2A.M1 | 2A.M2 | 2A.D1

1 You are playing for a local sports team and are looking to improve your fitness levels so that you can be more competitive in your sport. You have decided to design a safe and creative six-week training programme to improve your performance. You should:

- outline your personal goals, aims and objectives
- outline other relevant personal information
- outline two personal exercise adherence factors and two success strategies
- use this information to design a programme (including warm-up and cool down) that appropriately applies the principles of training.

2 To make sure your programme is appropriate for your needs, justify to your coach why you have designed your programme in the way you have.

Tips

- Remember to use SMARTER goals.
- Consider how realistic your aims and objectives are.
- Include your lifestyle and physical activity history, highlighting any strengths and areas for improvement.
- Include a completed medical history questionnaire and a description of any medical factors that could influence training programme design (such as recent injuries or asthma).
- Consider your attitudes and personal motivation to train, highlighting the positive and negative aspects of both.
- You will need to show that your programme is safe by showing that you are using the right equipment, following correct training techniques and taking into account your fitness and medical history.
- You will need to show that your programme is creative.

Implement a self-designed personal fitness training programme

Introduction

Safety is an important part of your training programme. You need to take into account the different safety factors when taking part in any sporting activity. You should also keep a training diary so that you can reflect on how the programme is progressing. This can help maintain your safety and ensure that the training programme is effective.

◤ Safely implement a personal fitness training programme

To implement your personal fitness training programme safely, you should:

Undertake appropriate training methods and complete planned sessions. You should use the descriptions of the different training methods in Unit 1: Fitness for Sport and Exercise, and in Topic A.4 to help you complete the training methods appropriately.

Use the correct technique through the different training methods and follow the manufacturer's instructions when using equipment. These two factors will mean that your training will be most effective with reduced risk of injury.

Always perform to the best of your ability to get the best out of your training sessions and lower the risk of injury.

Make sure you have the agreement of your teacher or coach if you plan to miss any training sessions.

Stay committed throughout the training programme. Think about the principle of reversibility – by missing sessions you are likely to start losing the gains made by training.

Wear correct kit.

Be aware of wider safety issues. For example, if exercising outdoors make sure that people know where you are training, that they have a way of contacting you and that the surface you will be training on does not pose hazards.

Take full responsibility for recording details for each training session. This will help you to see if your training programme is working.

Using a training diary to record each session

When keeping a training diary, you should record the following details:

- date, time and location
- aims and objectives for each session
- session duration
- type of training undertaken – selected methods/activities
- programme details (FITT)
- log of personal performance and achievements
- resources required, e.g. equipment
- the principles of progressive overload and details of how progressive overload has been achieved over the course of the programme
- programme intensity using percentage HRmax and RPE.

Measures for success

In your training diary, you should also describe the different measures for success. These include your motivation to train, how your programme has been adapted, achieving aims and overcoming barriers.

Motivation for training

When describing this part, include details in the diary of your feelings before, during and after each training session. For example, did you want to train, or did you feel that you had to train but couldn't really be bothered.

How the programme has been adapted

As your programme progresses, you will probably change it to ensure continued commitment to training; for example, using a new variety of activities/training methods. You should record in your diary when, how and why you adapted your training programme.

Achievement

Achievement against personal aims, goals or objectives should also be recorded in the training diary; for example, if you were able to lift your target weight in the gym or achieve your target time on a run.

Overcoming barriers

In this section of your training diary, describe how you overcame your barriers to training and issues/problems that you faced while training.

Reflect

If you highlighted poor motivation to train as a barrier as part of Assessment activity 5.1, how did you overcome this barrier before and during your training?

Just checking

1 What details should you include in your training diary for each session?
2 What factors should you consider when thinking about measures for success?

Review your programme

Getting started

Which factors might you consider to be strengths or areas for improvement after a training programme? How could you use this information to suggest future training recommendations?

Introduction

At the end of a training programme it is important to review its strengths and areas for improvement so that you can suggest and justify future training recommendations.

Review programme

It is important that you review your training programme before and after each training programme. Your reviews should show **strengths** and **areas for improvement**, as well as providing evidence of where you have modified the training programme to achieve personal goals.

Key terms

Strengths – areas of the training programme where personal aims and objectives have been achieved.

Areas for improvement – areas where training outcomes did not meet planned goals; for example, you planned to improve muscular strength but did not improve over the 6 weeks specified.

Training that uses more than one activity can provide welcome variety.

Future recommendations

When thinking about future recommendations, you should consider the areas for improvement first as these will still be your future training priorities. By thinking about the areas for improvement, you will be able to decide on your personal training needs and will be able to think about the use of different training methods where appropriate. For example, it may be that you have not improved your aerobic endurance as much as you would have liked because you didn't really enjoy the continuous running programme that you had set, so in future you would want to consider using a range of aerobic training methods (e.g. Fartlek training and interval training) and activities (e.g. alternating between running, swimming and cycling in different training sessions) to maintain your motivation and enjoyment.

How could you improve your training programme for the future?

Assessment activity 5.2   *Maths English*   2C.P5 | 2D.P6 | 2C.M3 | 2D.M4 | 2C.D2 | 2D.D3

You now need to safely implement your six-week training programme.

1 You should maintain a training diary to summarise outcomes and appraise your performance and progress throughout.

2 At the end of the six weeks, consider your strengths and areas for improvement, providing recommendations for future training.

Tips

- Record the main points about the outcomes of your training sessions.
- Keep a record of your strengths and areas for improvement throughout the training programme.
- When preparing recommendations for your future training, say how and why they would improve your performance.

Introduction

Behind every great sports performer and sports team is a great leader. Sports leaders are often the unsung heroes, the people who spot weaknesses and develop them, turning athletes into winning Olympians and teams into league or cup champions. It is the sports leader who plans physical activity sessions and steers the development of a performer's skills and techniques to meet aims and objectives. They often make key decisions at important times which change the fortunes of individuals and teams. It's a lot of responsibility, so a sports leader must be appropriately prepared and have had adequate experiences within their sport. At grass roots level sports leaders are vital in ensuring that young people remain interested and enthused.

In this unit you will be introduced to the basics of sports leadership and will be required to plan and deliver sports activity sessions. You will then evaluate your own effectiveness to determine if there are areas where you can further develop your abilities.

Assessment: You will be assessed by a series of assignments set by your teacher/tutor.

Learning aims

In this unit you will:

A know the attributes associated with successful sports leadership

B undertake the planning and leading of sports activities

C review the planning and leading of sports activities.

I have always wanted to be a swimming coach. My own coach was such an inspiration to me and I hope to share my own experiences with younger swimmers at my club. After completing this unit I know which attributes I need to develop in order to fulfil this ambition.

Megan, *17-year-old aspiring swimming coach*

Leading Sports
Activities

6

Assessment Zone

This table shows you what you must do in order to achieve a **Pass**, **Merit** or **Distinction** grade, and where you can find activities to help you.

Assessment criteria			
Level 1	**Level 2 Pass**	**Level 2 Merit**	**Level 2 Distinction**
Learning aim A: know the attributes associated with successful sports leadership			
1A.1 Outline the attributes required for, and responsibilities of, sports leadership	**2A.P1** Describe, using relevant examples, the attributes required for, and responsibilities of, sports leadership **See Assessment activity 6.1, page 163**	**2A.M1** Explain the attributes required for, and responsibilities of, sports leadership **See Assessment activity 6.1, page 163**	
1A.2 Describe the attributes of a selected successful sports leader	**2A.P2** Describe the attributes of two selected successful sports leaders **See Assessment activity 6.1, page 163**	**2A.M2** Evaluate the attributes of two successful sports leaders **See Assessment activity 6.1, page 163**	**2A.D1** Compare and contrast the attributes of two successful sports leaders **See Assessment activity 6.1, page 163**
Learning aim B: undertake the planning and leading of sports activities			
1B.3 Plan a given sports activity	**2B.P3** Plan two selected sports activities **See Assessment activity 6.2, page 173**	**2B.M3** Justify the choice of activities within the sports activity plan **See Assessment activity 6.2, page 173**	
1B.4 English Lead a component of a sports activity session, with guidance and/or support	**2B.P4** English Independently lead a sports activity session **See Assessment activity 6.2, page 173**	**2B.M4** English Lead a successful sports activity session **See Assessment activity 6.2, page 173**	
Learning aim C: review the planning and leading of sports activities			
1C.5 Maths Review the planning and leading of the warm-up, main component or cool down, describing strengths and areas for improvement	**2C.P5** Maths Review the planning and leading of the sports activity session, describing strengths and areas for improvement, and targets for future development as a sports leader **See Assessment activity 6.2, page 173**	**2C.M5** Explain targets for future development as a sports leader, including a personal development plan **See Assessment activity 6.2, page 173**	**2C.D2** Justify targets for future development as a sports leader and activities within the personal development plan **See Assessment activity 6.2, page 173**

English Opportunity to practise English skills

Maths Opportunity to practise mathematical skills

How you will be assessed

This unit will be through a series of assignments set by your teacher/tutor. You will be expected to show that you understand the attributes required for successful sports leadership using examples of successful sports leaders. You will also be required to plan two sports activity sessions, and then deliver one of these. On completion of the session you will be required to review your effectiveness as a leader by commenting on your strengths and areas for improvement.

Your assessment could be in the form of:

- a written report
- session plans with detailed justification of selected activities
- observation of you leading a session (or a component of a session)
- visual evidence of you leading a session (video/photographs)
- report of the outcomes of the session and review of session including a development plan.

Sports leaders and their attributes

Introduction

In this section, you will learn about the different types of leaders in sports and the **attributes** that sports leaders need in order to be successful.

Sports leaders

There are many types of leadership role in sport. Examples of sports leaders include sports coaches, fitness instructors, school/college coaches, and local and national club coaches. A sports leader's main aim is to encourage participation in sport and ensure that sports sessions are safe and well organised.

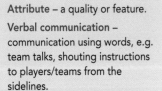

Figure 6.1 Types of sports leader

Attributes

Skills

Sports leaders need to develop certain skills if they are to be effective in leading sport and physical activity sessions.

Communication

Sports leaders use a variety of methods when communicating to participants in their sports sessions:

- **verbal communication** – e.g. giving technical instructions to sports performers
- **non-verbal communication** – e.g. facial expressions and bodily gestures
- **listening** – e.g. after asking a sports performer a question and requesting a response.

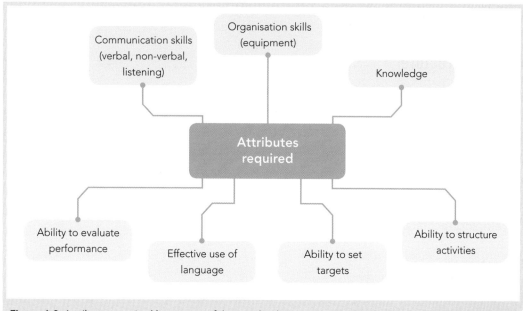

Figure 6.2 Attributes required by a successful sports leader

Research

1 For two sports, research the qualifications required to coach and lead different age groups and abilities. You may find this information under 'Education' on the website for the National Governing Body for each sport.

2 Present the information you find to the rest of your group.

The more effective your methods of communication the easier it is to get a variety of messages across to players, spectators, other coaches and officials when appropriate.

Non-verbal communication often helps sports performers read the mood of the sports leader.

Communication between the leader and performer should be a two-way process, supporting the development of knowledge for both.

Organisation of equipment

As a sports leader, you must have a clear understanding of the equipment you are going to need to deliver each sports or physical activity session or event. Prior to the session, you should make sure you have all the equipment prepared, check that it is in full working order and make sure that you are aware of how to use it in a safe and effective way.

Knowledge

Sports leaders should have a wealth of knowledge about the sport they are delivering, including:

- the technical and tactical demands of the sport
- the specific fitness requirements of the sport
- laws, rules and regulations of the sport
- the treatment of basic sports injuries and first-aid techniques.

As sports leaders develop, their knowledge will increase. It is a requirement in many sports that people involved in the organisation and planning of sports activity sessions attain sport-specific leadership and coaching qualifications.

An example of non-verbal communication. What do you think are effective and ineffective methods of communication?

CONTINUED ▶▶

⏵ Advanced skills

Activity structure

When delivering a sports session, it is important that you follow the correct format:

1 **warm-up**
2 **main component**
3 **cool down**
4 **feedback/debrief**.

You should ensure that each component of the session is safe, as well as effective in developing technical ability and/or tactical knowledge.

Target setting

When planning a session a sports leader will set out specific goals or targets. These are called the **aims** and **objectives**.

The leader will further develop these throughout a series of sessions, as his or her knowledge of the individual development needs of the performers increases.

Sports leaders should set short-term targets that need to be achieved by the end of the session. They should also set medium- or long-term targets to be achieved by the end of a series of sessions, by the end of a season, or over a longer period of time.

> **Key terms**
>
> **Aims** – what you want to achieve in your session.
>
> **Objectives** – how you are going to achieve your aims in the session.

What skills will a coach use when talking one-on-one with a sports performer?

Use of language

Successful sports leaders have a clear voice and use language that is appropriate for the performers they are working with. Through effective use of language you will develop:

- a rapport with and between the performers
- a high level of sport-specific knowledge (including technical and tactical knowledge and rules and regulations of the sport) between performers
- a sense of respect between performers
- the sports performance of individuals and teams.

When working with beginners you will need to use basic language to explain each activity. Language for elite performers will be much more technical. A good leader will increase performers' knowledge by explaining techniques, tactics, rules and regulations in a clear and concise way.

At all times, a good sports leader will think before speaking, to demonstrate respect for all people involved in the session or sports event.

Evaluation

Sports leaders should provide participants with feedback on their strengths and areas for improvement relating to their performance. However, they should also reflect on their own performance as a sports leader. The key to effective self-evaluation is honesty. It can be easy to identify what you have done well, but more difficult to comment on the things you haven't done well. Try to seek support from experienced sports leaders and coaches and learn from them. This will enable you to develop your weaknesses and enhance your effectiveness in leading sports activity sessions.

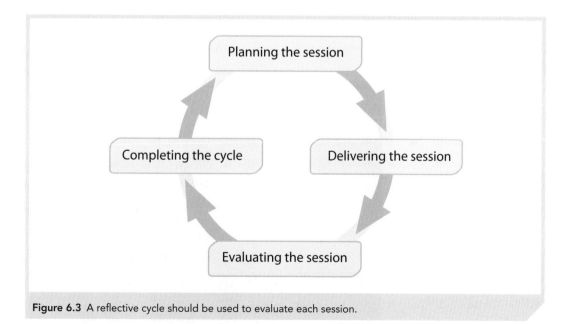

Figure 6.3 A reflective cycle should be used to evaluate each session.

CONTINUED ▸▸

Sir Alex Ferguson is famous for his leadership style. Can you think of positive leadership qualities he has?

Qualities

It is important that good sports leaders demonstrate a number of positive qualities. These will shape the relationships they develop with participants in the sessions they are leading.

Appearance

Sports leaders should take care of their appearance and dress appropriately for each session. As a sports leader, you are a role model – this involves wearing the right kit and behaving appropriately in each session, and ensuring that performers follow your lead by doing the same.

Enthusiasm

Good leaders must be able to combine innovative ways of delivering sports and physical activity sessions with:

- knowledge of the sport or activity
- effective communication
- leadership skills
- high levels of enthusiasm.

An enthusiastic and knowledgeable sports leader can leave a lasting impression on sports performers. When a sports leader is smiling and happy, this feeling often rubs off on the performers in the session.

Confidence

A sports leader should have the confidence to stand in front of performers and direct them towards achieving a target or goal. Confidence will develop as you increase your own experience and knowledge. This is a key quality for a sports leader.

| Activity 6.1 | Thinking about qualities for sports leadership |

Look at the image of Hope Powell (CBE), one of the most successful England football coaches.

1 Using the image, identify the leadership qualities she is showing.

2 Select your favourite sports leader who has led you in a sports or physical activity session. Comment on each of the following qualities:
  - appearance
  - enthusiasm
  - confidence.

3 Feed back your findings to the rest of the group.

4 Select three famous sports leaders from three different sports and describe how they demonstrate effective qualities when leading sports performers.

Hope Powell (CBE)

◢ Additional qualities

Leadership style

There are three identifiable sports leadership styles, which are outlined in Table 6.1.

Table 6.1 Characteristics, advantages and disadvantages of leadership styles

Leadership style	Characteristics	Advantages	Disadvantages
Autocratic	• Leader makes all decisions, and tells sports performers what to do and how to do it.	• Good for beginners when delivering basic skills and techniques.	• Only works on single skills in isolation. • Difficult to assess prior knowledge of performers.
Democratic	• Leader involves sports performers in the decision-making process, but makes the final decision on what is to be delivered in the session.	• Develops close relationships between leader and sports performers. • Develops communication and confidence of sports performers.	• Time-consuming. • May be problematic in large groups if there are many differing opinions.
Laissez-faire	• Performers make the decisions. • Sports leader is used as a mentor and helps the performers when appropriate.	• Helps develop self-confidence and decision-making skills of sports performers. • Can increase motivation of sports performers.	• May be a lack of structure to the sessions. • May take a long time to meet goals. • If leader does not intervene when necessary, performers could learn incorrect techniques.

In order to be a successful sports leader, you will be required to use all of these effectively. Different types of leadership suit different types of performers and different activities. The style you choose will depend on a number of factors, including the aim of the session (what is to be achieved), the performers within the session (how they work together) and how the performers react to different leadership styles (this may depend on their level). It is important to consider how every individual is going to be enhanced by the session.

Motivation

Our level of motivation can determine what we do (and possibly what we don't do). As a sports leader it is important to understand what motivates performers to participate in sports to ensure that they remain focused and achieve their goals.

There are two forms of motivation:

- **intrinsic motivation** – when a sports performer participates in an activity or sport for its own sake. They are motivated by the pleasure of the activity and the satisfaction or sense of accomplishment they feel from playing or participating.

- **extrinsic motivation** – this concerns the influence of things outside the athlete or activity, such as external rewards. An extrinsically motivated sports performer is motivated by external factors rather than the sport or activity. They play the sport with a desire to achieve something, such as a medal or prize.

CONTINUED ▶▶

José Mourinho is often seen as an extrovert. Do you agree?

Link

For more information on personality types see *Unit 3: The Mind and Sports Performance*.

Fabio Capello is often seen as an introvert. Do you agree?

Humour

It is important for sports leaders to have a sense of humour; this enables them to relate to the performers. Obviously it is important that laughter is only used at appropriate times. Performers' enjoyment is increased when they know their sports leader can share a joke with them.

Personality

Personality can be defined as the characteristics that make each individual unique. All sports leaders have their own individual characteristics and methods. It is important that sports leaders are confident and have the ability to plan and lead sport and physical activity sessions. Personalities fall into two categories: **introvert** and **extrovert**.

- **Introverts** are individuals who do not actively seek excitement and would rather be in calm or quiet places. In the world of sport introverts tend to prefer sports that require low levels of excitement but require high concentration levels and accuracy in their delivery.

- **Extroverts** are inclined to get bored quickly and are often poor at tasks that require a great deal of concentration. They constantly seek stimulation and excitement.

Activity 6.2 — Introvert or extrovert?

Make a list of ten famous sports performers. Place each one into a category: introvert or extrovert. Write the performer's sport in brackets after their name.

Introvert	Extrovert
Roger Federer (Tennis)	Usain Bolt (Athletics)

Make a list of your friends and complete the exercise again. Think about the characteristics of your friends and discuss with the group what makes them introverted or extroverted.

Just checking

1 What are the different methods of communication that should be used by sports leaders?

2 What is an aim?

3 Provide an example of an aim for any sports leadership session.

4 What is an objective?

5 What structure should a sports session follow?

6 Identify each stage of the reflective cycle.

WorkSpace

Luke Damas

Football coach

I have recently attained my Level 1 Award in Coaching Football and have been helping out with the under-11s at my own football club, alongside my old team coach, Hannah.

It first started when I went to watch my younger brother training – I wanted to play, as I always do when I see anyone playing football. However, Hannah would not let me play; I am more than five years older than my brother and much bigger.

Hannah did ask if I wanted to help her out with the team and I agreed. At first I really struggled with not playing and joining in, but Hannah taught me to constantly watch over the players in order to ensure they don't make mistakes or do anything silly. Similarly, Hannah has developed my ability to spot hazards and deal with potentially dangerous situations.

During a recent game one of the players was injured. As Hannah's assistant, I ran onto the pitch and spotted that the injury was much more serious than a normal kick to the shin. I panicked and shouted for Hannah to come over. She was very calm, and calmed me down as well as the player who was injured. She dealt with the incident appropriately and effectively – she ensured that the correct action was taken and that the player (I later found out he had broken his leg) was taken to hospital with a parent to support him. The rest of the players were kept away from the incident to ensure they were not distressed by the injury.

Think about it

1   When leading sports activity sessions, why is health and safety so important?

2   Can you think of a plan that you should follow when serious injuries take place on a football field, or within a competitive situation in your own sport?

3   What courses would you need to undertake to become a qualified first aider?

Responsibilities of sports leaders

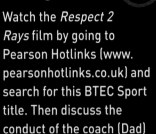
Key terms

Equality – treating everyone fairly.

Inequality – social disparity, e.g. inequality between the rich and the poor.

Prejudice – intolerance of or dislike for people based on, for example, race, religion, sexual orientation, age or disability.

Introduction

Sports leaders must fulfil a number of core and additional responsibilities. Every sports leader represents the sport they are delivering, so it is important that they do so with appropriate care and attention to all of the required areas of legislation. It is not always the sports performer who judges a sports leader, but possibly the club that the sports leader works for or the parents of children in the care of the leader.

Core responsibilities

Professional conduct

It is important that performers see their sports leaders conduct themselves in an appropriate manner. The expectations about leaders' behaviour come from the performers and spectators of the sport, as well as the people who have appointed the leader.

Sports leaders should promote participation in physical activity by providing participants with positive values, including playing within the rules of the sport.

Figure 6.4 Responsibilities of a sports leader

Equality

As a sports leader you will deliver sports and physical activity sessions to a range of performers with different abilities. Whatever their differences, you must provide all sports performers with the same opportunities to develop and improve their performance – this is what **equality** is about. Sports leaders should lead sport and physical activity sessions without any **inequality** or **prejudice** and must ensure all participants are treated equally and included in all of their sessions.

Activity 6.3   Code of conduct

Develop a code of conduct for all sports leaders to follow when leading sport and physical activity sessions.

Sports leaders are responsible for the health, safety and well-being of sports performers during the period of time in which they are under their supervision.

Health and safety

Sport is a physical activity and carries an element of challenge for all who participate. Achieving the challenges and targets set will demand a mixture of skill, fitness and coordination. The risk of accidents is always there, so the skill of identifying hazards that could cause accidents, and minimising the risk, is a key requirement when planning and leading sport and physical activity sessions.

Sports leaders have responsibility for sport performers during the period of time in which they are under their supervision; this includes the health, well-being and safety of participants. It is therefore important that a sports leader not only checks on the performers throughout the session to ensure they are safe and healthy at all times, but also makes sure they are always aware of risks and hazards that could cause injury.

Case study

As a sports leader at an athletics club you are shocked to be informed that during the previous week's training session an athlete was injured after being hit by a discus. After investigation, it seems that this happened because an athlete ran across the throwing area during the end of the training session in an attempt to get to the changing rooms before his friends. The club have taken this minor injury very seriously and would like to devise a strategy to ensure that incidents like this do not happen in the future.

1 Complete a five-point plan to be followed by every sports leader prior to the start of every session.

2 Develop a code of conduct for sports performers and sports leaders at the club with regards to health and safety.

3 Identify five hazards that could cause injury and the types of injuries that each hazard could cause.

4 Identify for each of the hazards the measures that could be put in place to reduce the risk of injury to participants and sports leaders who may be affected.

CONTINUED ▶▶

◤ Wider responsibilities

Insurance

Sports leaders must have appropriate insurance cover to participate in physical activity, and lead sports or physical activity sessions. They are responsible for the safety of all performers under their supervision. If a sports performer were to get injured the sports leader would be held responsible for the accident and might be considered negligent.

Child protection

Child protection has become a concern in sport and physical activity. When children are introduced to new people in new settings it is vital that a sports club keeps children safe and adheres to their statutory duties set out in legislation such as the Children Act (1989 and 2004). It is the duty of sports clubs to fulfil this responsibility.

Many sports clubs now complete police checks and ensure that sports leaders undertake child protection training via workshops on a regular basis.

Take it further

To find out more about child protection and sports leadership visit the NSPCC Child Protection in Sport Unit website. You can access this by going to Pearson Hotlinks (www.pearsonhotlinks.co.uk) and search for this BTEC Sport title.

Legal obligations

There are a number of legal requirements that can affect the work of a sports leader. It is your responsibility to know and understand the relevant legislation and all that you should be doing to follow it. Laws are passed by the government to support the safety of people who wish to undertake physical activity. The following Acts have been implemented by the government and are relevant to sports leaders at the time of publication:

- **Disability Discrimination Act 1995**: this act makes it illegal for anyone providing a service to discriminate against disabled people. This includes accessibility and provision in sport and physical activity.
- **Activity Centres (Young Persons' Safety Act) 1995**: this act requires that all centres offering adventure activities for children under the age of 18 are registered and licensed to HM Government's Adventure Activities Licensing Service. The requirements are that all staff possess specific qualifications, and follow specific operation and emergency procedures in their centre. It is also a requirement that the centre has the correct ratio of staff to children participating in any activity.

Rules and regulations

Link

See *Unit 2: Practical Sports Performance* for more information on the rules and regulations in sport.

When leading sessions it is important to promote the rules and regulations of the sport. As well as developing an individual's technical ability the session should also develop their knowledge of the game. Sports leaders should ensure that participants learn how to follow the rules and respect officials.

Sports leaders should promote friendship and respect for others.

Ethics and values

Ethical practice can be described as honest, fair and responsible conduct and actions. Values are ideas to which we attach worth or importance. Effective sports leaders should promote ethics and values within their sports sessions. The following principles should be encouraged:

- friendship
- respect for others
- playing with the right spirit
- equal opportunities
- fair play.

Assessment activity 6.1   2A.P1 | 2A.P2 | 2A.M1 | 2A.M2 | 2A.D1

You have been approached by Sport Makers, an initiative within your local council that supports the development of leadership skills in sport in your local area. They have asked you to develop a leaflet for all potential sports leaders about the attributes required to be an effective sports leader.

1 Consider the skills, qualities and responsibilities that leaders must adopt and use to be effective when leading sports sessions.
2 Select two sports leaders of your choice and compare the attributes they have that make them so successful as leaders.

Tips
- For each sports leader, describe the attributes they are demonstrating when they are successfully leading a sports activity session.
- Identify the strengths of your chosen sports leaders, and also the areas where they might have weaknesses they would benefit from developing. Give evidence for each of your statements.
- Consider the attributes the leaders share, as well as those that are different.
- 'Evaluate' means bringing together your information and reviewing it to reach a conclusion. Do this by identifying the strengths of your chosen sports leaders, and also the areas where they might have weaknesses that they would benefit from developing. Give evidence for each of your statements.

Sports activity sessions and their components

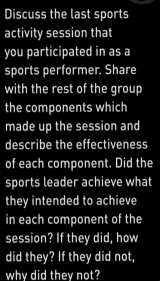

Getting started

Discuss the last sports activity session that you participated in as a sports performer. Share with the rest of the group the components which made up the session and describe the effectiveness of each component. Did the sports leader achieve what they intended to achieve in each component of the session? If they did, how did they? If they did not, why did they not?

Introduction

Sports activities can take many different forms; for instance, they can involve individual or team sports, or fitness activities such as circuit training. In this unit you will be required to deliver all, or a component of, a sports activity session to a specific group of performers and demonstrate your ability to plan and lead it effectively.

Components of sports activity

Warm-up

Every sports session should start with a warm-up to prepare the sports performers both physically and mentally.

The warm-up should last for at least 10 minutes. It should take a methodological approach which:

- initially increases body heat and the respiratory and metabolic rates
- stretches the muscles and mobilises the joints that will be used in the session
- includes rehearsal and practice of some of the activities that are required in the sport.

Main components of the session

The session could include a variety of activities depending on the aims and objectives. If these are to introduce or develop a specific skill, the sports leader will need to include technical drills and skill practices, depending on the sport and skill being covered in the session. If the aims and objectives are to develop a specific aspect of fitness, the session will have to include appropriate fitness activities.

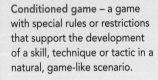

Key term

Conditioned game – a game with special rules or restrictions that support the development of a skill, technique or tactic in a natural, game-like scenario.

The main body of the session often includes a competitive element. Some sports leaders will use this to develop the skill or component of fitness covered earlier in the session. To do this a sports coach may choose to use a **conditioned game**. For example, if the aim of the session is to develop short passing in football, the coach may choose to condition a competitive game at the end where a team can score a goal for completing ten or more consecutive passes.

Cool down

At the end of the session a sports leader should ensure that all participants spend an appropriate amount of time cooling down. The aim of this is to bring the body gradually back to the pre-exercise condition. If performed correctly, a cool down should prevent muscle stiffness and injury and improve flexibility, provided stretches are performed correctly and controlled effectively by the coach.

Discussion point

Look at the image of a sports performer stretching. Stretching should be an integral part of all sports leaders' sessions.

1 Select a sport that you enjoy participating in.

2 For that sport, identify all of the muscles required for effective participation.

3 As a group, for each muscle select a stretch that can be used in a warm-up to prepare the muscle for physical activity and in a cool down to help return the muscle to its pre-activity state.

Just checking

1 What should the main components of a warm-up be?

2 Provide an example of a skill development drill.

3 What is a conditioned game/practice?

4 Provide an example of an effective cool down for a volleyball session, which is fun and appropriate for young children.

Planning sports activities

Introduction

In order to ensure that sports participants develop in every session, it is important that a sports leader plans each session thoroughly. Such plans should be both inclusive and flexible.

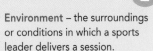

Key terms

Environment – the surroundings or conditions in which a sports leader delivers a session.

Outcome – the results of the session: what happened and the aims and objectives that were met in the session.

Participants

Prior to planning your sport or physical activity session you should collect information about your group. This should include:

- group size
- age
- ability of performers
- gender mix
- interests and previous experience
- medical information
- specific needs of participants.

The session plan that you design will have to be realistic for the needs and aspirations of the performers you will be delivering your session to. Sports leaders will deliver sessions to a range of participants, including children, young adults, the elderly and disabled performers.

Resources

When planning any sports or physical activity session, the equipment is often essential in meeting the aims and objectives of your session. Prior to sports or physical activity sessions the sports leader should check the availability of the equipment and facilities and ensure that these are safe and appropriate for the session.

When using a new venue it is important that the sports leader is aware of the **environment** in which they are delivering their session, including emergency procedures and the location of the changing rooms and toilets.

Another important resource to consider when planning a sports or physical activity session is time. The amount of time which you have to deliver the session is very important and can determine the activities that are included.

When planning a sports activity, a sports leader must check the availability and suitability of the facilities they want to use.

Aims and objectives

All sports sessions should have aims, which should be clearly stated on your session plan and agreed with participants at the start of the session. Each aim should be an expected **outcome**, which will be achieved by all or some of the sports performers within the session. For example, 'I want everyone in this session to be able to throw a ball by the end of it.' You may aim towards different outcomes for different sports performers within the session.

To achieve your aim, you will need to set some objectives. These should be written clearly on your session plan and should express how you will meet each of your aims.

Health and safety

Health and safety is the most important responsibility of a sports leader.

It is important that risk assessments and all appropriate checks are carried out before you complete your session or event to ensure that it runs as smoothly as possible without risk of injury to any of the sports performers or other leaders involved. Safety checks should be carried out throughout the session.

When planning an event where there may be large numbers of participants, every possible occurrence should be considered. Sports leaders must have knowledge of basic first aid and understand what action to take if serious injuries occur during the session. It is your responsibility to ensure that someone who has a relevant first aid certificate is available during the delivery of your event and that they have appropriate equipment and resources to carry out this role.

Activity 6.4	Health and safety planning

Put together a 10-point safety checklist that you will use before any sport or physical activity session.

Risk assessment

A risk assessment is a careful examination of the various hazards within the environment in which your session is taking place, including the equipment you are using to deliver the session. It should identify the level of risk posed to the sports performers, the spectators and you as the sports leader. Within the risk assessment you should ensure that you identify all the hazards and clearly plan what actions will be taken to minimise the risks.

Informed consent

Before running any sports session, the sports leader should ensure that all sports performers who are participating in the session have completed a **consent form** to confirm that they:

- are able to participate in the session
- know what is required from them within the session
- have consented to their participation if old enough (if below the age of 18 this will need to be done by a parent/carer); this is indicated by a signature on the form
- have provided you with any details of medical issues that may prevent them from participating, and any injuries or underlying health issues.

 Key term

Consent form – used to obtain permission to participate in a physical activity session (this must be completed by a parent/carer for all sports performers under the age of 18).

Leading a session, and measuring success

Getting started

Think of the last successful sports or physical activity session you participated in. What made it successful?

Can you think of five factors you will need to consider in order to lead a successful session?

Introduction

When leading a sports or physical activity session, it is important to stick to the session plan and use a variety of methods to measure the success of the session.

Link

For more information on each of the attributes required to lead a sports activity session successfully, refer back to *Topic A.2*.

Demonstration of attributes

When leading an activity session or sports event a sports leader will demonstrate skills, qualities and responsibilities that have already been covered in this unit. The leader should ensure that the session flows and provide a variety of activities for the sports performers, and most importantly ensure that performers are safe at all times. This should be measured through effective planning and preparation, pre-activity checks and through the sports leader monitoring the performance of the athletes during the session.

The sports leader should set out the aims and objectives of the session at the start and for each activity, and clearly state the rules and regulations. When possible the sports leader should relate these to the rules and regulations of the sport being coached to reinforce knowledge and develop the participants' understanding.

An important skill that sports leaders have to master is communication. Sports leaders will have to be able to communicate effectively to ensure that their group understands the instructions provided and can follow them to support their own development.

A sports leader should be able to clearly communicate tactics to sports performers.

Link

For more information on how to apply each of the responsibilities and wider responsibilities within a sports activity session successfully, refer back to *Topic A.3*.

Completion of core and wider responsibilities

When leading a sports activity session you should ensure that all of the core responsibilities and wider responsibilities required to be a successful sports leader are appropriately applied.

A sports activity session should be delivered using methods that are as visual as possible. Sports leaders should demonstrate to learners what they want them to do. The sports leader should have sufficient knowledge of the technical requirements of the skills to demonstrate the correct methods to the learners. A sports leader who is unable to carry out the demonstration because of injury or any other reason should still carry out a demonstration but using another member of the group, or another coach or sports leader who is available. A sports leader who is unable to carry out the demonstration should describe each key factor of the technique and discuss its importance in the application of the skill.

The sports leader should ensure that the session is aimed at the correct level and that the language used is appropriate to the participants. The session must be exciting and enjoyable for the performers but should also develop them, by providing them with appropriate guidance and feedback throughout the session. The leader should ensure that all participants are monitored throughout the session and that positive feedback is used to encourage performers.

Activity 6.5   Demonstrating skills

Look at the image of a sports leader assisting with the demonstration of a skill to a group of children. Select four skills from a selected sport and discuss with your group the correct technical method of demonstration of each skill to a group of sports performers.

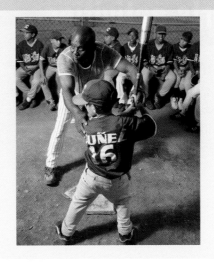

Measures of success

It is important as sports leaders that we measure the success of the sessions that we deliver. The methods we use to measure success can take many different forms.

Figure 6.5 Measures of success by sports leaders

Within your session plan it is important that you clearly state which measures of success you will be using.

Just checking

1 What are:
   a The skills required to lead a successful sports activity session?
   b The advanced skills required to lead a successful sports activity session?

2 What are:
   a The qualities required to lead a successful sports activity session?
   b The additional qualities required to lead a successful sports activity session?

3 What are:
   a The core responsibilities when leading a successful sports activity session?
   b The wider responsibilities required to lead a successful sports activity session?

Reviewing the planning and leading of sports activities

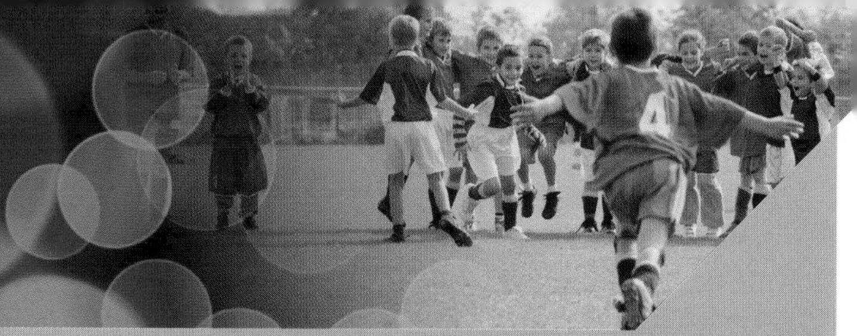

Introduction

After the completion of a session or event a sports leader should invite participants to give feedback. This feedback can then be used by the sports leader to identify components of the session that went well and components of the session that may require development in future.

Key term

Feedback – the information you obtain from yourself and others which reflects on your performance. In this instance the feedback you obtain will be the opinions of others about your performance as a sports leader.

It is key for your development as a sports leader that you obtain feedback from others, including your teachers/supervisors and any observers of the session who may be able to provide you with guidance and support. The feedback you obtain from experienced sports leaders/coaches can be used to improve and develop your performance.

It is important that, on completion of the session, you also complete a self-analysis. This is where you give your own comments on the session. The questions you should ask yourself when completing a self-analysis are as follows:

1. Did I meet the aims, targets and objectives of the sessions as listed within the session plan?
2. Did the participants enjoy the session?
3. Was the session risk-free and did I ensure that nobody got injured?
4. Did I demonstrate all of the attributes required to lead a sports leadership session successfully?

Methods

A range of methods can be used to generate feedback. These could include:

- questionnaires
- comment cards
- observation records
- direct verbal feedback.

The method you use to collect feedback from participants in the session will be different from the method you use to collect feedback from the observers.

You could ask the performers how they felt the session went (direct verbal feedback), but this method may not always generate honest feedback; the use of a questionnaire may generate more genuine opinions.

Please tick your answers

Did you enjoy the session?

Did you enjoy the warm-up?

Did you enjoy the drills in the session, e.g. dribbling between cones, shooting into the hockey net?

Did the sports leader communicate clearly?

Did the sports leader demonstrate clearly what you had to do in the session?

Did you feel that your performance improved in the session?

What extra activities would you like to have done in the session?

....

....

....

....

....

Figure 6.6 After a sports event you could obtain feedback from performers using a questionnaire.

Reviewing sports activities

Within your group, complete four different warm-ups.

To assess the effectiveness of each warm up, obtain feedback from each of the participants.

Prior to the session, you should develop a variety of methods to obtain feedback from the participants after each of the warm-ups.

Ensure you use a different method of feedback for each of the sessions.

Once all of the feedback has been collected, discuss which methods collected the most honest and useful responses.

Strengths and areas for improvement

After receiving feedback from participants and observers you should then conclude what you felt were the strengths of your session/event and what parts you would like to develop and improve on.

Once you have gathered all of the feedback from the session you should consider the following components and complete your review of the session.

- What sort of feedback did you get about your successful demonstration of attributes when leading the session?
- With reference to the feedback, how do you think you managed each of the responsibilities required to lead a sports activity session successfully?
- How effective was the planning for the sports activity session?
- What was the content of the sessions like – what did different people like, and why do you think they liked some parts but not others?
- How organised did people think the session was? Did you ensure that everyone was safe at all times?
- What did you achieve within the session, and what did the performers achieve within the session?

When developing areas for improvement it is important to ask yourself a number of questions:

- What went well in the session?
- What went wrong in the session?
- Why does a particular component of the session need developing?
- What did other people say (feedback) about this part of the session?
- What can I do to develop this part of the session?

CONTINUED ▸▸

Targets for development

After you have considered what your strengths and areas for improvement are when leading sports sessions, you should then set a series of targets to support your own development as a sports leader.

SMARTER targets

When setting yourself targets you should use the SMARTER model:

- **Specific** – make the target as precise and detailed as possible.
- **Measurable** – consider the methods used to measure your performance against the targets.
- **Achievable** – goals should be attainable and should be relevant to the sports performer.
- **Realistic** – appropriate targets that can be met within the timescales set.
- **Timed** – ensure you set yourself a deadline to have achieved your targets by.
- **Exciting** – the targets that are set should motivate and challenge the individual or team.
- **Recorded** – progress towards the attainment of each target should be recorded.

Development plan

A development plan is a formal way of planning methods to enhance your ability as a leader. By making a record of activities, you will be able to measure the progress you are making over time.

A development plan should have clear aims and objectives – these can be short-, medium- and long-term goals, but importantly should all be attainable. You should consider using the SMARTER method to plan your aims.

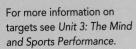

Link

For more information on targets see *Unit 3: The Mind and Sports Performance*.

Key term

Barriers – obstacles that may prevent someone from participating in a sport or physical activity. For example, money – if a young child does not have enough money for golf clubs they will be unable to play golf.

Within your development plan, list and justify all the activities and opportunities you feel would develop you as a sports leader. These may include specific training courses or qualifications to develop your skills. They may even include observing and supporting other, more experienced, sports leaders at other sports clubs.

Within your development plan it is also important that you include a summary of the potential **barriers** that may prevent you from achieving your aims, objectives and goals. These might include lack of time, lack of money, lack of transport or lack of availability of courses, for example.

Sports leaders should always be setting targets for their development.

Assessment activity 6.2 | *English Maths* | 2B.P3 | 2B.P4 | 2B.M3 | 2B.M4 | 2C.P5 | 2C.M5 | 2C.D2

You have been asked to help out with your school's Year 6 Taster Day, where pupils from local primary schools come in to see what different subjects are like at your school. The Head of PE has asked you to plan and support some of the PE taster sessions.

1 Prepare a session plan for:

- a circuit session

- an activity session for any team game.

You should give reasons for your choice of activities.

2 The Head of PE was particularly impressed with your circuit session plan and would like you to lead this session. Carry out the session with a group of pupils.

3 Review your planning and leading of the circuit session. What were your strengths? Are there areas where you could improve? Set some targets for your future development as a sports leader using a personal development plan, and give reasons for these.

Tips

For Task 1, ensure your plans include:

- information about the participants' age, ability, gender and specific needs; aims and objectives; resources; and health and safety considerations

- a warm-up, main activity/components of activity, and cool down

- a risk assessment

- an informed consent form for each participant

- different methods to collect feedback from the performers in the sessions to help you evaluate your performance as a leader and the success of the session.

For Task 2:

- lead the activity confidently, knowing the requirements of each component of your session

- demonstrate a variety of attributes and responsibilities throughout the session and lead independently

- on completion of the session, obtain feedback from all participants.

For Task 3:

- remember to refer to the feedback you obtained from your teacher and participants in your session.

- present your areas for improvement as aims and objectives

- produce a development plan which highlights your goals and the SMARTER targets you are going to follow in order to develop as a sports leader

- include opportunities and activities which could develop your leadership attributes and responsibilities, justifying how each opportunity or activity will develop your skills.

Glossary

1-RM – the maximum amount of weight that you can lift in a single repetition.

A

Achievement motivation – an individual's motivation to master a task and achieve excellence.

Acromion process – the outer end of the scapula, forming the highest point of the shoulder.

Active stretching – stretches performed by a sports performer on their own. The performer applies force to stretch and lengthen the muscles.

Adaptation – changes made within the body to increase its ability to cope with training loads.

Adenosine triphosphate (ATP) – a molecule that is the only useable form of energy in your body.

Adrenaline – a hormone that prepares your body for exercise.

Adversity – an unfavourable or negative experience that can happen during sport.

Aerobic – using oxygen.

Aerobic endurance – the ability of the cardiorespiratory system to work efficiently, supplying nutrients and oxygen to working muscles during sustained physical activity.

Agility – the ability to move quickly and precisely or change direction without losing balance or time.

Aims – what you want to achieve in your session or by the end of the training programme.

Anaerobic – not dependent on oxygen.

Anaerobic exercise – exercise that doesn't use oxygen as the main way of releasing energy.

Anterior auxiliary line – the crease at which the top of your arm, when hanging down, meets the chest.

Anticipatory rise – an increase in your heart rate before you start exercising.

Anxiety – the level of worry or nervousness an individual experiences.

Areas for improvement – areas where training outcomes did not meet planned goals.

Attitude – how positive or negative you generally feel about something.

Attribute – a quality or feature.

Autocratic – a leader who makes all decisions, and tells sports performers what to do and how to do it.

B

Balance – the ability to maintain centre of mass over a base of support. There are two types: static balance and dynamic balance.

Ballistic stretching – involves making fast, jerky movements, usually in the form of bouncing or bobbing through the full range of movement.

Barriers – obstacles that may prevent someone from participating in a sport or physical activity.

Bioelectrical impedance analysis (BIA) – method used for measuring body composition.

Blood plasma – the water-based component of blood.

Blood pooling – the process in which blood is no longer forced to return to the heart after exercise has stopped suddenly and so stays in the legs.

Blood pressure – the force exerted by blood against the walls of the blood vessels.

Body composition – the relative ratio of fat mass to fat-free mass (vital organs, muscle, bone) in the body.

Bone density – the amount of minerals (such as calcium) in your bone, sometimes referred to as bone mineral density.

Bradycardia – a decreased resting heart rate.

C

Calcium – a mineral that is important for maintaining bone health.

Candlestick technology – video software which shows a sports performance in slow motion.

Capillarisation – new capillaries developing and existing capillaries becoming more efficient to help the movement of blood.

Cardiac hypertrophy – increasing size and strength of the heart muscle.

Cardiac output – the amount of blood pumped out per minute.

Cardiorespiratory system – a combination of the cardiovascular and respiratory systems.

Cartilage – a tissue that protects the ends of bones.

Circuit training – moving from one exercise to another at a series of stations.

Cognitive anxiety – the mental effects of anxiety.

Collagen – a protein that is important for bone formation.

Competitive situations – events where more than one sports performer competes to achieve a set goal.

Component – a part of something.

Conditioned game – a game with special rules or restrictions that support the development of a skill, technique or tactic.

Conditioned practices – practices with special rules or restrictions that support the development of a skill, technique or tactic in a natural, game-like scenario.

Consent form – used to obtain permission to participate in a physical activity session.

Constant-resistance exercises – exercises in which the amount of resistance for a muscle/muscle group remains the same throughout the repetition.

Continuous skills – skills that have no obvious beginning or end and can be continued for as long as the performer wishes.

Continuous training – training method that involves keeping a steady pace over a long distance.

Coordination – the ability of parts of the body to work together to move smoothly and accurately.

Core muscles – muscles that are responsible for maintaining good posture.

Creatine phosphate (CP) – a molecule that can quickly be converted to ATP for energy.

Criteria – a standard by which a sports performer is judged.

D

Dartfish technology – video software which shows a sports performance in slow motion.

Democratic – leader who involves sports performers in the decision-making process, but makes the final decision on what is to be delivered in the session.

Diastolic pressure – pressure that results when the heart relaxes and fills with blood.

Discrete skill – a skill that has a clear beginning and end.

Dominant side – an individual's dominant/preferred side of the body.

Dynamic balance – maintaining balance whilst in motion.

Dynamic stretching – performing activities that are similar to the sporting movements and will be needed during a game or event.

E

Elastic strength – ability of a muscle to contract quickly and overcome resistance.

Energy system – method of converting nutrients to energy.

Environment – the surroundings or conditions in which a sports leader delivers a session.

Enzymes – the catalyst for chemical reactions that release energy for exercise.

Equality – fair treatment of everyone.

Evaporation – process by which a liquid turns into vapour.

Exercise adherence – how well you stick to your exercise programme.

Extrinsic motivation – external factors that influence motivation, such as trophies.

Extroverts – people who are outgoing and comfortable in the company of others.

F

Fartlek training – Swedish training method involving a variety of intensities and terrains.

Fatigue – tiredness.

Fatty acids – produced from the breakdown of fat. Fatty acids are converted to ATP for energy.

Feedback – the information you obtain from yourself and others which reflects on your performance.

FITT principle – Frequency, Intensity, Time, Type.

Fixed-resistance machines – weight training equipment where a weight/fixed amount of resistance is used.

Flexibility – having an adequate range of motion in all joints of the body.

Free weights – a weight that is not attached to another machine or device.

Frequency – the number of training sessions you complete over a period of time.

G

Gaseous exchange – the exchange of oxygen and carbon dioxide between the lungs and blood.

Glycogen – a form of carbohydrate stored in the liver and muscles.

Glycolysis – the process of converting glycogen/glucose to ATP for energy.

Goal – something that you want to achieve.

H

Heart rate – the number of times the heart beats per minute.

Heart rate training zone – the lower and upper heart rate you should be training between.

Height stadiometer – equipment used for measuring height.

Hyaline cartilage – cartilage found on joints that absorbs synovial fluid.

Hypertension – high blood pressure (greater than 140/90 mmHg).

Hypertrophy – an increase in the size of skeletal muscle.

I

Imagery – a technique used to enhance self-confidence by picturing yourself being successful.

Imaginal experiences – imagining personal performances are successful.

Incline press-ups – a press-up exercise where the hands are placed on a raised surface.

Individual differences/needs – each individual's different ability levels, goals, physical attributes, medical history and training activity preferences.

Inequality – social unfairness, e.g. inequality between the rich and the poor.

Intensity – how hard you are working.

Intention – planning to do something.

Interactional view – the explanation that suggests behaviour and motivation are shaped by a combination of traits and the social environment.

Interaction – when sports performers communicate effectively with the aim of attaining a joint goal.

International Governing Body (IGB) – an organisation responsible for the promotion and development of a particular sport at an international level.

Interval training – training method that involves alternating work periods with rest and recovery periods.

Intrinsic motivation – internal factors that influence motivation, such as enjoyment.

Introvert – a person who does not to actively seek excitement and prefers calm environments and tasks that require lots of concentration.

Invasion games – a game in which teams have to get into their opponents' area in order to score.

Isolated practices – training drills and skill-specific exercises.

Isometric – muscular action in which tension develops but there is no change in muscle length and no joint movement.

L

Lactic acid – a natural by-product of exercise that is produced when carbohydrates are broken down to release energy.

Laissez-faire – sports leader who lets performers make decisions and helps them when appropriate.

Long-term (LT) goals – what you want to achieve in the long term.

M

Maximal fitness test – requires the participant to make an 'all-out' maximal effort.

Medium-term (MT) goals – goals that give progressive support towards achievement of long-term goals.

Metabolic activity – the body's way of releasing energy so that it can be used for exercise.

Micro-tears – tiny tears in muscles that are necessary 'damage' for a muscle to get bigger and stronger.

Mitochondria – the part of the muscle that produces energy aerobically.

Motivation – the internal mechanisms and external stimuli that arouse and direct behaviour.

Motive to achieve – achievement motivation that means you will eagerly accept challenges and strive for success.

Motive to avoid failure – an individual's efforts to avoid failure.

Muscular endurance – the ability of muscles contract over a period of time against a light to moderate fixed-resistance load.

Muscular strength – the maximum force that a muscle or muscle group can produce.

Musculoskeletal system – a combination of the muscular and skeletal systems.

N

National Governing Body (NGB) – an organisation responsible for the promotion and development of a particular sport at a national level.

Nomogram – special chart used to process data and obtain the correct units of measurement for the interpretation of test results.

Non-verbal communication – communication without using words, e.g. facial expressions and bodily gestures.

Normative data table – data table that presents the usual results given from testing a specific group of people.

O

Objectives – how you are going to achieve your aims in the session.

Observing – watching people to see which traits or behaviours they display.

Official – a representative of a National Governing Body who applies the rules of a specific sport in competitive situations.

Officiate – to administer the rules and control the game, race or match.

Olecranon process – bony projection at the elbow.

Optimal – the best, or most favourable.

Osteoporosis – a condition in which you have brittle bones.

Outcome – the results of the session.

Outcome goals – goals that focus on the outcome of an event, such as winning a race.

P

Passive stretching – requires another person or object applying an external force, which causes the muscle to stretch.

Performance accomplishments – previous accomplishments that increase your belief in future performances.

Performance goals – objectives that focus on the athlete developing their own performance, and that make comparisons with their own performance.

Personality – the sum of characteristics that make a person unique.

Pliable – able to stretch and change shape without breaking.

Plyometric – training that develops sport-specific explosive power and strength.

Posture – a position that the body can assume.

Power – the work done in a unit of time. It is calculated in the following way: Power = Force (kg) × Distance (m) / Time (min or s).

Practicality – how easy a fitness test is to carry out in terms of the costs involved, time available and equipment requirements.

Prejudice – intolerance or dislike of people of a specific race, religion, sexual orientation, age, disability, etc.

Principles of training – factors that you must take into account to ensure that your training will be successful.

Process goals – goals that focus on what needs to be done to improve performance.

Progressive overload – increasing your training workload gradually so that your body keeps adapting.

Proprioceptive Neuromuscular Facilitation (PNF) – an advanced form of passive stretching that inhibits the stretch reflex that occurs when a muscle is stretched to its full capability, so that an even greater range of movement can occur.

Psychological core – the most stable and innermost, 'real' part of the personality.

R

Reaction time – time taken for a sports performer to respond to a stimulus.

Regulations – rules in sport that are controlled by an authority (a National Governing Body).

Reliability – consistency of fitness test results.

Repetition maximum (1-RM) – the maximal force that can be exerted by a muscle or muscle group in a single contraction.

Repetitions – the number of times you perform a single exercise such as a biceps curl; often abbreviated to 'reps'.

Rest and recovery – time to allow the body to repair and adapt, and for the renewal of body tissues.

Re-synthesise – to reproduce ATP.

Reversibility – the reversal of training effects if you stop training, or the intensity of training is not sufficient to cause adaptation. Also known as de-training.

Role – the actions and activities assigned to or required or expected of a person.

Role-related behaviours – the least stable part of the personality, which is influenced by the environment.

S

Sanction – a penalty which is awarded against a sports performer for breaking a rule.

Self-confidence – the belief that a desired behaviour can be performed.

Self-efficacy – self-confidence in a specific situation.

Self-talk – a technique used to improve self-confidence by telling yourself that you will be successful.

Serial skill – a series of individual skills that together produce an organised movement.

Sets – a group of repetitions; for example, an experienced strength trainer may complete three sets of six reps.

Short-term (ST) goals – goals set over a short period of time, between 1 day and 1 month.

Situational view – the explanation that suggests behaviour is shaped by our social environment.

Situation-centred view – the view that motivation is determined by the situation we find ourselves in.

Skill – something that we learn how to do.

Somatic anxiety – the physical effects of anxiety.

Specificity – how specific training is to the individual's preferred sport, activity, or physical/skill-related fitness goals.

Speed – distance divided by the time taken, measured in metres per second (m/s).

Sport – an activity involving physical exertion, skill, competition and rules.

Spotter – a person who watches/helps a participant during a particular weight training exercise.

Stable – people who are not easily affected by their emotions.

State anxiety – temporary anxiety due to the nervous system becoming activated.

Static balance – maintaining balance in a stationary position.

Static stretching – slowly stretching a muscle to the limit of its range of movement and then holding the stretch still for 10 to 20 seconds.

Strength endurance – a muscle's ability to perform a maximum contraction and repeat over a long period of time.

Strengths – areas in which performance is consistently successful.

Stroke volume – the amount of blood pumped by the heart in one beat.

Submaximal – exercising below an individual's maximal level of physical effort.

Submaximal fitness test – fitness test in which the participant performs the test at less than their maximal effort.

Synovial fluid – a fluid that lubricates and nourishes a joint.

Systolic pressure – pressure that results when the heart contracts.

T

Tactics – strategies or actions planned to achieve a desired goal.

Third umpire – an off-field umpire who makes the final decision in questions referred to him by the two on-field umpires.

Tidal volume (TV) – the amount of air inhaled and exhaled with each breath.

Time – how long you train for.

Trait anxiety – a personality factor that is characterised by consistent feelings of tension and apprehension due to the nervous system being continually activated.

Trait-centred view – the view that motivation is determined by our personality, needs and goals.

Traits – personality characteristics that can be used to predict or understand behaviours in different settings.

Trait view – the explanation that suggests our behaviour is based on personality traits.

Trigger – something that starts off a particular behaviour.

Type A personalities – people with a high competitive drive who are quite prone to anger and hostility.

Type B personalities – people who are generally laid back and of a quiet disposition.

Typical responses – the way that we usually respond to different situations.

U

Umbilicus – belly button.

Unstable – people who have a relatively changeable mood and is easily affected by their emotions.

V

Validity – the accuracy of the fitness test results.

Variation – variety in your training programme to prevent boredom and maintain enjoyment.

Vasoconstriction – narrowing of your arterioles.

Vasodilation – widening of your arterioles.

Verbal communication – communication using words, e.g. team talks.

Verbal persuasion – used by teachers, coaches and peers to persuade you that you can be successful.

Vicarious experiences – using modelling or demonstrations to develop self-efficacy.

Video analysis – using video footage to review practices and games, and improve performance.

Video referee – replaying footage in sports before making or revising a decision.

Views of personality – explanations that have been given to help us understand why we behave in particular ways.

Vital capacity – the amount of air that you can forcibly expel from the lungs.

VO$_2$ max – the maximum amount of oxygen uptake.